Not Without Thorns, by Ennis Graham

You are holding a reproduction of an original work that is in the public domain in the United States of America, and possibly other countries. You may freely copy and distribute this work as no entity (individual or corporate) has a copyright on the body of the work. This book may contain prior copyright references, and library stamps (as most of these works were scanned from library copies). These have been scanned and retained as part of the historical artifact.

This book may have occasional imperfections such as missing or blurred pages, poor pictures, errant marks, etc. that were either part of the original artifact, or were introduced by the scanning process. We believe this work is culturally important, and despite the imperfections, have elected to bring it back into print as part of our continuing commitment to the preservation of printed works worldwide. We appreciate your understanding of the imperfections in the preservation process, and hope you enjoy this valuable book.

NOT WITHOUT THORNS.

NOT WITHOUT THORNS.

A Story.

BY

ENNIS GRAHAM,

AUTHOR OF "SHE WAS YOUNG AND HE WAS OLD," ETC.

"D'ailleurs qui est-ce qui atteint son idéal?"—V. Hugo.

IN THREE VOLUMES.
VOL. III.

LONDON:
TINSLEY BROTHERS, 18, CATHERINE STREET, STRAND.
1873.

[*All rights of Translation and Reproduction are reserved.*]

LONDON:
SAVILL, EDWARDS AND CO., PRINTERS, CHANDOS STREET,
COVENT GARDEN.

CONTENTS

OF

THE THIRD VOLUME.

CHAP.		PAGE
I.	ROMA'S SENTIMENTS	1
II.	HOME	27
III.	VISITORS, EXPECTED AND UNEXPECTED	52
IV.	BY THE SPRING	89
V.	THE LAST STRAW	122
VI.	FRIENDS IN NEED	154
VII.	ROMA TO THE RESCUE	184
VIII.	O SI SIC OMNIA!	217
IX.	INSUPERABLE OBSTACLES	244
X.	FROM THE GATES OF THE GRAVE	267

NOT WITHOUT THORNS.

CHAPTER I.

ROMA'S SENTIMENTS.

And if thy wife and thou agree
But ill, as like when short of victual.
T. CARLYLE, *The Beetle.*

Il m'est impossible de ne point vous féliciter.
Les Misérables.

CAPTAIN CHANCELLOR had been away more than a fortnight. During that time Eugenia had received several short notes from him, most of which contained pretty much the same information, that business matters at Halswood had proved more complicated than he had expected, that there was so much to arrange and settle he found it impossible to return to Winsley as quickly as he had intended, but that he trusted Eugenia was comfortable and happy with his sister; indeed he felt sure she would be so, and so on. There was never any allusion to the little scene which had occurred the morning he left, and from the tone of his letters it was so evident to Eugenia that long before the remembrance of it had ceased acutely to distress her, her husband had forgotten all about it, that she on her side refrained from mentioning it.

"It will be best never to refer to it," she thought to herself. "Only when Beauchamp returns I shall be doubly careful, so that he may see how anxious I am to please him even in trifles."

More than once it had happened that the same post which brought Eugenia a short note from her husband brought Mrs. Eyrecourt a much lengthier epistle from him. This was the case one morning about this time. It was a dull, close day, and Eugenia, always sensitive to such influences, had been hoping earnestly while dressing that her letters might bring news of Beauchamp's speedy return. The disappointment was great when she opened the thin letter addressed to her, dated this time from Bridgenorth, and found that another fortnight must pass before he could rejoin her.

"I came on here yesterday," he wrote, "having got through the most pressing part of the business at Halswood, and hoping to get my leave, which is up next week, extended at once, for my papers were sent in last week. But I find as I am here I must stay till the middle of the month, when I hope to get away for good."

"Another whole fortnight," sighed Eugenia. "Oh dear, how I do wish Beauchamp had let me wait for him at home instead of here. It would have been so different. I could have seen Sydney every day."

The tears rose unbidden to her eyes at the thought of the contrast between such a state of things and her present position, but she checked them back quickly, as looking up she saw that Gertrude was watching her. She went on reading her letter, though she already knew its few words by heart, holding it so as to prevent her sister-in-law seeing how short it was.

"You have a letter from Beauchamp, I suppose," said Gertrude. "So have I—a tremendous one, isn't it?" she fluttered half a dozen sheets through her fingers for Eugenia's benefit. "I really can't read it all till after breakfast. It is all about Halswood. I was anxious to know how he finds everything, and so Beauchamp has sent me all the details—the particulars of the whole, the rents of the great farms, how the entailed *money* property is invested, and I don't know all what, but all so interesting to me of course, knowing it so well. It isn't exactly *women's* business certainly, but then I have had a good deal of business to look after in my time. The womenkind of men of property should be able to help their husbands and sons, you know."

She went on speaking as if Eugenia were an ordinary uninterested visitor, either really forgetting, or affecting to do so, that to the woman before her of all women in the world Beauchamp Chancellor's interests must be the closest and dearest. The blood seemed to boil in the young wife's veins, but recent experience had not been lost upon her, and her power of self-control had increased greatly in the last few weeks.

So she answered, quietly, "Yes, they certainly should, and so should other people's wives too. It is one of my father's hobbies that women of all classes should be better educated, so that they may be better able to help men, and sometimes to work alone even."

"Oh, I wasn't referring to that sort of thing. I hate all that talk about women's rights, and so on: it is very bad taste," exclaimed Gertrude, contemptuously. "I don't know, and don't want to know anything about the women of any class but my own. But of course there is nothing unfeminine in managing one's own business matters when one understands how. I have almost been brought up to it, you see, always having lived on our own land—and I certainly need all I know now, with

Quintin's long minority before me and Beauchamp at the head of the Halswood affairs too. He is sure to be always consulting me. That reminds me I must be quick, for I must answer his letter before luncheon, and it will take me a good while."

She went on with her breakfast, but happening to move aside the large envelope of her brother's letter, her eye fell on another, which, with a little exclamation, "From Roma, I didn't expect to hear from her to-day," she took up and read.

"Roma is coming home to-morrow," she announced to Eugenia, in a minute or two. "A week sooner than she expected."

"Is she really? I am so glad!" exclaimed Eugenia, thankful for any interruption to the present uncongenial tête-à-tête with her sister-in-law, doubly thankful that it came in the shape of a person she was already inclined to like.

"Why, have you ever seen her? Oh yes, to be sure, she stayed a night at Wareborough and was at your marriage. I forgot you had seen her," said Mrs. Eyrecourt.

"I saw more of her last winter," said Eugenia, "at the time she stayed a week or so with Mrs. Dalrymple—just when Beauchamp first came to Wareborough,"—"and I met him in the fog, and all the world was changed to me," was the unspoken conclusion of her sentence.

"Oh yes; I think I remember something about it," said Gertrude, indifferently. "Dear me, was that only last winter? What changes in so short a time!"

She sighed softly. Somehow the sigh was irritating to Eugenia; her instinct told her that the reflections accompanying it would not have been gratifying to her to hear. But she little guessed what they actually were. "If I had foreseen it all," thought Gertrude, "I certainly would not have been so eager to prevent Beauchamp's marrying Roma" (for that this would have come to pass had *she* chosen to encourage it, no power on earth, no protestations of the young lady herself, however earnest, could ever make Mrs. Eyrecourt cease to believe): "it would have been far—oh, infinitely better than *this!* Though of course even now nothing could have been so perfectly suitable as Addie Chancellor," and then poor Gertrude sighed.

"I am very glad too' Roma is coming," she said, amiably, becoming conscious suddenly of the audibleness of her sigh, and feeling a little shocked at herself. "By-the-bye, Eugenia, she sends her love to you and hopes to find you still here."

"Thank you," replied Eugenia, rather coldly. But in her heart she did feel very glad of the news. She hoped many things from Roma's advent. Roma was kind and womanly and sensible. She had known Beauchamp all his life, and must understand him thoroughly. *Her* advice Eugenia would not feel inclined to scorn. Roma could never be patronizing; hers was by many degrees too large a nature for anything so small. And though clever mostly in a worldly sense perhaps—clever and satirical and dreadfully *au fait* of everything—

Eugenia did not feel in the least afraid of her. Though she had been everywhere and seen everything and knew everybody; though her education had reached far, in directions where Eugenia Laurence's had never even begun, yet she was not conventional, not spoilt, not incapable of sympathy with the great human universe outside her own immediate sphere. Such at least was Eugènia's ideal Roma—Roma with the bright dark eyes, ready words, and kindly smile.

And Mrs. Eyrecourt was very glad too. Roma would help her, she hoped, to entertain this pretty, uninteresting wife of Beauchamp's, whom she found such heavy work; for Roma was great at this sort of task—she had quite a knack of getting stupid people to talk, discordant ones to agree, doing it too, with so much self-forgetfulness and tact, that the credit of this comfortable state of things usually fell to Gertrude's own share.

"Such a charming hostess! so unselfish and considerate for every one."

It was not much to be wondered at that

so warm-hearted and unselfish a creature had not found the charge of her husband's young sister a burdensome one. And as, even in this crooked life, goodness sometimes is recompensed, Gertrude Eyrecourt met with her reward. Everybody—*her* everybody—praised her for her sisterly behaviour to homeless Roma; and Roma herself, whose capacity for gratitude was both wide and deep, thanked her constantly, though tacitly, by doing everything in her power to please her, resolutely refusing to see her smallnesses and selfishnesses, admiring her and respecting her judgment—and now and then too by determinedly disagreeing with her.

Both Mrs. Eyrecourt and her guests found their hopes fulfilled. Roma's return improved the state of things immensely. She came home in great spirits, having enjoyed her visit far more than she had expected, yet declaring, and with evident sincerity, somewhat to Eugenia's surprise, that she felt delighted to be at home again.

"Who do you think was my travelling

companion part of the way?" she said, when the three ladies were sitting together the first morning after her arrival. "He got in at Marly, and saw me into my train at the junction—he was going on to town. Do guess who it was—he is a friend of yours, Eugenia. Why, how stupid you both are! You are generally so quick at guessing, Gertrude."

"I!" exclaimed Mrs. Eyrecourt, looking up, as if aware for the first time that Roma had been speaking to her. "I beg your pardon, I thought you said the unknown was a friend of *Eugenia's*."

"Well, and if I did, is the world so big that by no conceivable chance two people living at opposite ends of the country could happen to have any mutual acquaintances?" said Roma. "To hear you speak, Gertrude, any one would think you had never been five miles from home. Like a nun I remember seeing when I was a child, in a convent in Switzerland, who thought, but wasn't quite sure—the mere idea even of such an adventure seemed to overawe her—

that when she was quite a little girl she had once been at Martigny, six miles from home. Why, Gertrude, I thought you prided yourself on being something of a cosmopolitan. Were you never at a place that long ago, when nobody but Miss Burney's heroines ever went anywhere, used to be called Brighthelmstone, and did you never dine with certain friends of yours there, who never get new dresses unless they are guaranteed to be of the fashion of twenty years ago, dear old souls?"

She spoke playfully, but there was a sharpness in her raillery which Mrs. Eyrecourt did not love. She could not endure being laughed at, and she felt annoyed with Roma for making fun of any of *her* friends, be they never so funny, all of which Roma knew, and had dealt out her words accordingly, for she had not been half an hour at home before she knew exactly how the wind blew as regarded the young wife, and she was on the alert to show Gertrude she need not look to her for sympathy in her prejudice.

But to Eugenia it was actual pain to

witness the annoyance or discomfiture of another. A sort of instinct made her try to change the conversation.

"Did you say that the Swiss nun had never in her life been anywhere?" she asked Roma. "Why had she been always in a convent? I never knew children could be sent to convents except as pupils."

"This girl was an orphan, and she had some money, and she had come to look on the convent as her home," said Roma; "she wasn't quite a lady; her father had been a rich farmer. I daresay she was happy enough, but it made a great impression on me as a child. It seemed so dreadful to be shut in between those four high walls when the world outside was so beautiful. I shouldn't have pitied her half so much if the convent had been in an ugly place."

"I don't know," said Eugenia, with a dreamy look in her eyes; "I think it would be something to have the sky and mountains to look out at if one were miserable."

The expression of her face struck Roma with a slight pain. It was not thus she had looked on her wedding-day, even when blinded with the tears of her farewell. Through those tears Roma had been able to pronounce her "perfectly happy."

"Is it Gertrude's fault, I wonder," thought Roma, with quick indignation, "or can she be stirring already in her slumber? And only six weeks married!"

But it was not Roma's way to dwell on unpleasant suggestions. The meeting troubles half way was an amusement which had never much recommended itself to her. So she answered brightly—

"Miserable, why should we think about being miserable? But all this time you are forgetting my travelling companion. As you wont guess who he was, I suppose I must tell you. It was Mr. Thurston, your brother-in-law's brother, Eugenia. The stranger, the new arrival from India, Gertrude, that we met at dinner at the Mountmorrises'."

"I was just thinking it must be he. He goes up and down that line so much. Did not you like him very much, Miss

Eyrecourt? I do exceedingly. And he is so clever and thorough. The only thing not nice about him is, he is a little—funny —I don't know what to call it."

"Funny? Do you mean humorous?" said Roma, looking at her with some amusement. "It did not strike me particularly."

"Oh no," replied Eugenia. "I don't mean that at all. I mean he is a little odd—uncertain. Sometimes he is so very much nicer than others. He gets queer fits of stiffness and reserve all of a sudden, and then one can make nothing of him. But oh," she exclaimed, checking herself suddenly, "I shouldn't criticise him in this way, for he has been so very good to me."

"I don't think you have said anything very treasonable," said Roma. "I can understand what you mean. He is a sensitive man—almost too much so. He looks as if he had had troubles too, though he is cheerful and practical enough. There is something about him unlike most of the men one meets—they are as a rule so very like each other, or else there is something about me which draws out the same sort of remarks from nearly every young man I meet."

"Really, Roma, I wish you would not talk such nonsense," said Gertrude, rising as she spoke. "I do think you should be more careful in what you say. You are getting into a way of thinking *you* can do or say what you like, which strikes me as the reverse of good taste. I confess I do not like your travelling all the way from Marly with a person of whom you know next to nothing. I hardly even remember meeting this Mr. Thurston at the Mountmorrises', and whether we did or not, that sort of introduction entails no more."

"But you forget that I said he was a connexion of Eugenia's, Gertrude," said Roma, quietly but very distinctly.

Mrs. Eyrecourt's tone softened.

"I did not notice what you said particularly," she replied, as she left the room. "Of course Eugenia will know I did not intend to be so rude as to speak disparagingly of any of her friends."

Roma smiled. "All the same, Gertrude, like many other people, *is* rude when she is cross," she remarked to Eugenia, for they were now by themselves. "Eugenia," noticing the puzzled expression of her companion's face, "why do you look so 'funny?' Are you shocked at me?"

"No," said Eugenia, "but I am not sure that I quite understand you."

"I am not worth much study, I assure you," said Roma, contentedly. "You will understand all there is to understand very soon. Suppose we go out a little. By-the-bye, doesn't that child trouble you? I saw her out there with you for such a time this morning."

"Floss," said Eugenia, "trouble me? Oh no. I like her. I should have been very dull without her."

"So you have been dull? I was afraid of it. I saw the look on your face when I said how glad I was to be back at Winsley again."

"Oh dear! I wish I could keep looks from my face," exclaimed Eugenia, pathetically. "Please forget about it. I should be so sorry to look as if I were not happy here. Beauchamp is so anxious that Mrs. Eyrecourt and I should get on well. He is very fond of his sister, unusually so, isn't he?"

"So he should be," replied Roma. "He owes her so much. So do I. She has been very good to us both."

"How?" asked Eugenia. "Of course I know she cares for Beauchamp, and—and takes great interest in him and all that, but still I don't quite know how you mean."

Roma looked surprised. "Has Beauchamp never told you how Gertrude has all her life been almost like a mother to him?" she said. "And to me too," she added. "I wonder he never told you."

"There has been so little time," said Eugenia, hesitatingly; "but I wish you would tell me. I want to understand things better."

There were no secrets involved. Roma was ready enough to give Beauchamp's wife a little sketch of the past. When it was finished Eugenia sighed.

"Thank you," she said. "I am glad to know it; I wish I had known it before. Perhaps it might have given me a different feeling to Mrs. Eyrecourt, and I might have managed to make her like me. As it is, I fear she does not. Oh, Roma," she went on, for the first time addressing Miss Eyrecourt by her Christian name—"oh, Roma, I wish I understood better. I am afraid I am not fit for the life before me. People seem to look at things so differently from what I fancied. I don't always understand Beauchamp even. I vex him without in the least meaning it. You know him so well, do you think you could help me at all? I am so terribly, so miserably afraid of his coming to think he has made a mistake."

The large brown eyes looked up beseechingly into Roma's; the piteous, troubled expression went straight to Roma's heart.

"You poor child!" she exclaimed impulsively, but checking herself quickly she went on in a different tone.

"You must not be afraid. Things always seem strange and alarming at first. Try and take them more lightly and don't be too easily daunted. I *do* know Beauchamp well, and I can assure you that, like many men, his bark is worse than his bite. You are more likely to annoy him by trying too much than too little to please him. He likes things to go on smoothly, and he can't understand exaggerated feeling of any kind. I don't think he is difficult to please, but he has got a certain set of ideas about women and wives—many men have, you know, but they modify in time. Only I suppose it is necessary to some extent to *seem* to agree with one's husband whether one does thoroughly or not—just at first, you know, before people have got to understand each other quite well."

"I am afraid that sort of thing would be very difficult to me," said Eugenia, sadly. "You see, I have always been accustomed to saying all I felt, to meeting sympathy wherever I wanted it. In some things I found it in my father; in others in my sister."

"You have been exceptionally happy," said Roma.

"Yes," returned Eugenia, "I have indeed. We always see our happiness most clearly when we look back. I fear I have been too tenderly cared for. Perhaps," with a faint laugh, "perhaps I am a little spoilt."

Roma smiled, but did not answer immediately. They were walking slowly up and down the terrace. Suddenly she turned to Eugenia with a question.

"Do you dislike the idea of Halswood—of living there, I mean?"

"Yes," answered Eugenia, frankly, "I do *very* much. I dislike the whole of it—the being rich, and all that."

"Would you really rather Beauchamp had not succeeded to the property?" asked Roma again, with a glimmer of amusement in her dark eyes.

"*Far* rather," returned Eugenia, with much emphasis.

"You extraordinary girl!" exclaimed Roma, now laughing outright; "what *would* Gertrude think if she heard you?"

"Perhaps she wouldn't believe me," said Eugenia, sagely. "But it is quite, quite true. Still I would not say so to her. I hardly think I would say so to Beauchamp even. It is the sort of feeling that he could hardly —that very few people could enter into."

"Very few indeed, I should say," replied Roma. "But, Eugenia, do you know I think you must try to get over the feeling. Solemnly, I assure you that I should have felt far more anxious about your future—yours and Beauchamp's I mean — had he remained poor. You don't know what it is. You don't know how very few people can resist the deterioration of that struggling, pinching life."

"We should not have been so very badly off," said Eugenia, far from convinced that she was mistaken.

"Yes, you would," persisted Roma; "for Beauchamp's tastes are all those of a rich man. He is so fastidious, and as a bachelor he has been able to indulge his fastidiousness to a great extent. Oh no, no, you are quite mistaken, Eugenia! I assure you you should be very thankful you are rich. It takes "—" a very different man to Beauchamp to make a good *poor* husband," she had it on her lips to utter, but stopped in time. Eugenia did not notice the interruption. She seemed to be thinking deeply.

"It seems to me so much more difficult than being poor," she said. "But you must know some things much better than I. I will try to think it is best."

"Yes, do, it will give you a much better start," said Roma, cheerfully. "And remember my advice, to take things lightly and not to be too sensitive. Not very lofty sentiments, are they? But there's some sense in them. Everything seems to be compromise, after all. Nobody is quite good or quite bad, and most people and most lives are made up of a great many littles of both. That is the extent of the philosophy to which my four-and-twenty years' experience has brought me?"

"It is very sad, *I* think," said Eugenia.

"But it might be worse?" suggested Roma.

Then they both laughed, and whether or no Roma's philosophy much commended itself to her, Eugenia certainly went about with a lighter heart and brighter face than had been hers during the last few weeks.

And the latter part of Mrs. Chancellor's visit to Winsley certainly proved a notable exception to the old proverb that "three are no company," for the three ladies were very much better company than the two had been, and Eugenia no longer counted the days to her departure, and openly expressed her hopes that when Beauchamp returned he would arrange to stay a little while with his sister; which expression of cordial feeling naturally gratified Mrs. Eyrecourt, and disposed her to regard her young sister-in-law in a more favourable light. Roma looked on and smiled, and enjoyed the present comfortable state of things, thinking to herself nevertheless that it was not on the whole to be regretted that the two counties respectively containing Halswood Hall and Winsley Grange were at a considerable distance from each other.

Captain Chancellor came back a fortnight after Roma's return, and a week later he took his wife to her new home. They did not travel thither by way of Wareborough, as Eugenia had hoped, but this disappointment she made up her mind to bear with philosophy. And Beauchamp, who had acted by his sister's advice in the matter, appreciated his wife's good behaviour to the extent of promising that once they were settled at Halswood, and had got the place into some sort of order, she should invite her father and Sydney and Frank to come to visit her in her own home. Eugenia mentioned this to Sydney in her next letter, but the smile with which the curate's wife read the message was a rather sad one.

"Dear Eugenia!" she said to himself; "I am afraid she is going to be far away from us—farther than she or any of us thought. But I trust she will not miss us."

CHAPTER II.

HOME.

*And sometimes I am hopeful as the spring,
And up my fluttering heart is borne aloft,
As high and gladsome as the lark at sunrise;
And then, as though the fowler's shaft had pierced it,
It comes plumb down, with such a dead, dead fall.*
Philip Van Artevelde.

IT was late in the evening of an August day when Captain Chancellor and his wife reached Halswood. Beauchamp had been anxious to complete the journey at once without any halts by the way, but to do this it had been necessary to leave Winsley very early in the morning, in consequence of which Eugenia was very tired. A certain excitement had kept her up during the first part of the journey, an excitement arising from mingled causes, but of which the anticipation of the glories of Halswood about to be revealed to her was a much less considerable one than would have been generally credited. Till they had passed Marly Junction, the ugly familiar station where everybody coming south from or going north to Wareborough and Bridgenorth always changed carriages, Eugenia had not been without a childish hope that she might catch sight of some home face; Frank perhaps, or more probably his brother, or not impossibly her father even. A sort of warm thrill of pleasure passed through her at the thought; it was more than two months since she had seen any one of the friends among whom her nineteen years of girlhood had been passed, and before her marriage she had never been away from her father's house for more than a fortnight—some amount of home-sickness was surely to be excused. All the way to Marly she felt as if she were going home in reality; the sight of a tall chimney, the dirty smoke-begrimed red of the streets of brick houses of the first little manufacturing town through which they passed made the tears come into her eyes. Her husband noticed their dewy appearance and remonstrated with her on the folly of sitting close beside the window, "with that abominable smoke and filthy smuts flying in." He got up and shut the window, remarking as he did so that railway lines to civilized places should really not be cut through these atrocious manufacturing districts; he trusted nothing would ever necessitate his entering Wareborough or Bridgenorth or any of these Wareshire towns again.

Eugenia said nothing, and changed her seat to the opposite side of the carriage as she was bidden. She had felt no temptation to confide to her husband the real cause of the emotion he had not even imagined to be such, but her eyes did not immediately recover themselves, and Marly once left behind, her spirits fell. Every mile of the unfamiliar country through which their journey now lay seemed to increase her painful sense of loneliness and strangeness.

"Oh," thought she, as they at last reached Chilworth, the nearest point to

Halswood, "oh, if only this were Bridgenorth, and we were going to the little house, or even to the lodgings we used to talk of living in there, and Sydney perhaps waiting to welcome us."

The tears got the length of dropping this time. She made no effort to conceal them, for by now it was too dark for her husband to see her face.

No sensation of any kind was perceptible at the little station on their arrival. Under the circumstances, of course any demonstration of rejoicing at the home-coming of the new lord of the greater part of the adjacent soil would have been the extreme of bad taste, and there was nothing by which a stranger could have guessed that the lady and gentleman who got out of the train and quietly passed through the station-gate to the carriage waiting outside were persons of more than ordinary local importance, save perhaps a certain extra obsequiousness on the part of the very unofficial-looking station-master, and a somewhat greater than usual readiness to bestir himself on the part of the solitary porter. Mrs. Chancellor, however, was far too self-absorbed to notice anything of the kind; it had never occurred to her to think of herself and her husband as objects of interest or curiosity to the outside world, and had the joy bells been ringing and bonfires blazing she would probably have turned to her companion with an inquiry as to the cause.

There was a momentary delay as she was getting into the carriage—Captain Chancellor turned back to give some additional instruction respecting the luggage. Eugenia standing waiting could not fail to notice that the brougham was a new one, and that everything about it, including the deep mourning livery of the men-servants, was perfectly well-appointed.

"What a nice carriage this is, Beauchamp," she said, when the door was shut, and they were rolling smoothly and swiftly away.

"Yes," he replied, not ill-pleased by her admiration; "I wrote for it when I first came down here. There was nothing fit for use. Herbert Chancellor never brought any carriages down here—not of course that they would have been mine if he had. Yes, it is a first-rate little brougham. Did you notice the horses? Oh no, by-the-bye it was too dark."

"I did not notice them. The lamps lighted up the carriage, and drew my attention to it. The horses were more in the shade. Not that I should venture to give an opinion on them. You know how dreadfully ignorant I am of such things."

"You will soon pick up quite as much knowledge of the kind as you need. I loathe and detest 'horsy' women. Roma even, if she were any one but herself, I should say had a shade too much of that sort of thing. But on the other hand, of course, it doesn't do to be in a state of utter ignorance about such matters."

"No, oh no," said Eugenia. "I quite know how you mean. I want to understand a little more about a good many things that I have not come in the way of hitherto."

Beauchamp's tone had been pleasant and encouraging. Eugenia's impressionable spirits began to rise. If she could but be sure of always pleasing her husband! If she could but feel that in all difficulties, great and small, she might appeal to him, certain of sympathy, certain of encouragement! It might come to be so—married life she had often heard, was not to be tested by the outset. Circumstances so far had certainly been somewhat against her. It might be that this coming to Halswood, so dreaded by her, was to be the beginning of the life of perfect union, of complete mutual comprehension which she had dreamt of.

A glow of new hopefulness seemed to creep through her at the thought—from very intensity of feeling she remained silent, wishing that she could find words in which to express to her husband a tithe of the yearning devotion, the ardent resolutions ready at his slightest bidding to spring into life. In a minute or two he spoke again.

"Are you tired, Eugenia?" he said. "What makes you so silent?"

There was a slight impatience in his tone. He wanted her to be bright and eager, and delighted with everything. He had by now almost got over his fear of "undue or underbred elation" at her good fortune, on his wife's part, and when alone with him some amount of demonstrative appreciation of what through him had fallen to her share, would not have been objectionable. But, as was usual with her, when carried away by strong feeling of her own, Eugenia perceived nothing of the restrained irritation in Beauchamp's voice.

"Tired," she said, with a little start, "oh, no; at least I may be a little tired, but it isn't that that made me silent. I was only thinking."

Her voice quivered a little. A sudden fear of hysterics came over Captain Chancellor. Some women always got hysterics when they were tired, and Eugenia was so absurdly excitable. A word or a look at any moment would make her cry,

"Thinking," he said, half rallyingly, half impatiently; "what about? Nothing unpleasant, I hope? though there certainly is no counting on women's caprices."

"I can't possibly tell you *all* I was thinking," she began, still speaking tremulously. "I was thinking how I do hope we shall be happy together in this new life, how I trust you will be pleased with me always, how I hope you will let me come to you with my little difficulties and anxieties, and—and that we may be at one always in everything, and not grow apart from each other. Oh, I can't half say what I feel. I think—I think, I sympathise a little with the wife in the 'Lord of Burleigh,' I feel frightened and ignorant, and a little lonely. But oh, Beauchamp, if you will help me— don't you remember that beautiful line—

> And he cheered her soul with love.

If we always keep close together, I shall not regret anything."

By this time she was in tears. Beauchamp was no great reader of poetry. He "got up" what was wanted for drawing-room small talk, and that was about all. But, as it happened, he knew the poem—the story of it, at least, to which she alluded, and had more than once made great fun of it.

"Catch any woman of the lower classes being such a fool. Founded on fact, not a bit of it. She died of consumption, you may be sure," was the opinion he had expressed.

So, being a little "put out" to begin with, and by no means in the humour for a sentimental scene—tears, and all the rest of it—Eugenia's somewhat incoherent speech, the allusion at the end of it especially, met with by no means a tender or sympathising reception.

"Really, Eugenia," he began, and at the sound of the two words all the new hopefulness, the revived tenderness, the warmth died in the girlish wife's heart—a cold, dull ache of disappointment, relieved but by the more acute stings of mortification and wounded feeling, setting in, the same instant, in their stead. "Really, Eugenia, you choose very odd times for your fits of—

I really don't know what to call it — exaggerated sentiment, as you object to 'gushingness.' We haven't been quarrelling that I know of, and I have no intention of doing so. What you mean by talking of 'not regretting' anything, I don't know in the least. I hate maudlin sentiment, and that poetry you are so fond of stuffs your head with it. For goodness' sake, try to be comfortable, and let me be so. No one expects impossibilities of you—you talk as if I were an unreasonable tyrant. If anything could 'drive us apart,' as you call it, it would be this sort of nonsense, and these everlasting tears."

He had paused once or twice in this speech, but Eugenia remained perfectly silent, and this irritated him into saying more than he intended, more than he actually felt, and the consciousness of the harshness of his own words irritated him still further. Still Eugenia did not speak. He let down the carriage window on his side impatiently, thrust his head out into the darkness, then drew it in, and jerked up the glass again. Eugenia did not move—he glanced at her. The tears he had complained of had disappeared as if by magic; her face, in the uncertain light of the carriage lamps, looked unnaturally white and set, the mouth compressed, the eyes gazing straight before them. It was really too bad of her to behave so absurdly, thought Beauchamp, feeling himself not a little aggrieved. Still, he wished he had not spoken quite so strongly.

"Eugenia," he began again, "do try to be reasonable. You take up everything so exaggeratedly. You know perfectly well I have no wish to hurt you. But really it is not easy to avoid doing so. Living with you is like treading on egg-shells."

Then she turned towards him with a look in her eyes which he had never seen in them before—a look which the sweet wistful eyes of Eugenia Laurence had never known, a look which should have made her husband consider what he was doing, what he had done.

"It is a terrible pity you did not find out my real character before," she said, "before it was too late. As it is too late, however, no doubt the best thing you can do is to tell me plainly how I can make myself the least disagreeable to you. You shall be troubled by no more 'maudlin sentiment,' or tears. So much I can promise you."

Then she became perfectly silent again.

Captain Chancellor gave a little laugh.

"I am glad to hear it," he said, with a slight sneer. "And, by Jove! what a temper she has after all," he thought to himself. "They are all alike, I suppose, all the world over. They all want a tight hand. But I flatter myself I know how to break them in."

Then he hummed a tune, drew out his watch and looked what o'clock it was, fidgeted with the window again, all with an air of perfect indifference, which he imagined to be his actual state of mind. But far down in his heart there was a little ache of self-reproach and uneasiness. Had Eugenia turned to him now with tearful eyes and broken words, little as he might have understood her feelings, he would certainly not have repulsed her.

Just at this moment the carriage turned in at the Halswood lodge. There was an instant's stoppage, while the heavy iron gates were opened, then they went on again, even more swiftly and smoothly than before.

"We are only a quarter of a mile from the house now," said Captain Chancellor. "You should see the lights from your side."

"Oh, indeed," said Eugenia, indifferently, turning her eyes listlessly in the direction in which he pointed, thinking that she would not care if an earthquake were suddenly to swallow up Halswood and everything connected with it, herself included; yet determined to hide all feeling— to appear as unconcerned as Beauchamp himself. "Ah, yes, I see them over there. I hope they will have fires," with a little shiver.

"Fires?" repeated Beauchamp. "After

such a hot day. Why, it is oppressive still. You can't be cold, surely?"

"Yes, I am," she said, "very;" and as she spoke, the carriage drew up under the pillared portico, which Captain Chancellor had pronounced so desperately ugly the first time he came to Halswood, and in another moment Eugenia's feet had crossed the threshold of what was now her home.

Three or four servants were waiting in the hall. At first sight Mrs. Chancellor imagined them to be all strangers to her, but in another moment, to her delight, she recognised in the face of a young girl standing modestly somewhat in the rear of the others, the familiar features of Barbara's niece. Mrs. Eyrecourt had not succeeded in her design of substituting a more experienced lady's maid in the place of Eugenia's protégée. Something had been said about it, but in the pressure of more important arrangements Captain Chancellor had allowed the matter to stand over for the present, and it had been arranged that

Rachel should be sent to Halswood the day before her mistress's arrival, but in the absorption of her own thoughts Eugenia had for the time forgotten this, and the pleasure of the surprise was great.

"Oh, Rachel!" she exclaimed with effusion, darting forward and shaking hands eagerly with the young girl—"I am so pleased to see you. Did you come yesterday, and how did you leave them all? How is papa? And Miss Sydney — Mrs. Thurston, I mean?"

"They are both very well, indeed, ma'am," said the girl, flushing with pleasure at the friendly greeting—her spirits had been somewhat depressed since her arrival; the great, empty house, the few servants, all middle-aged or old, had seemed strange and cold to Barbara's niece; "I went to see Mrs. Thurston the last thing the night before I left—there is a letter waiting for you from her upstairs that she told me to put in your room—and Mr. Laurence, ma'am he wished me to——"

"Eugenia," said Captain Chancellor's

voice from behind his wife, "Eugenia, if you are not *very* particularly occupied, will you spare me a moment?"

She had vexed him again, but in the softening influence of the home news, the sound of the dear home names, Eugenia's better self was again uppermost. There was no resentment or haughtiness in her tone or manner as she turned quickly towards her husband.

"Oh, I am so sorry," she exclaimed; "I was so pleased to see Rachel and hear about them all at home, that I——" But she said no more, for glancing at Beauchamp, she saw that her words had deepened rather than lightened the look of annoyance on his face.

"Mrs. Grier," he said, addressing an elderly person in black silk, tall, thin, stiff, and yet depressed-looking, who came forward as she heard her name. "Eugenia, this is Mrs. Grier. Mrs. Grier has been at Halswood for I don't know how many years. How many is it?" turning to the housekeeper with the pleasant smile that so lighted up his somewhat impassive face.

"Thirty-three, sir," replied Mrs. Grier, thawing a little, " and more changes in the three than in all the thirty."

"Yes, indeed," said Eugenia, kindly, shaking hands with the melancholy house-keeper. "You must have had a great deal to go through lately."

"I have, indeed, ma'am. Three funerals in a year, and all three the masters of the house," answered Mrs. Grier, shaking her head solemnly. "It isn't often things happen so in a family. But all the same, ma'am, I wish you joy, you and my master, ma'am."

"Thank you," said the two thus cheerfully addressed.

Eugenia felt almost inclined to laugh; but Captain Chancellor hardly relished the peculiar style of Mrs. Grier's congratulation.

"It's time the luck should turn again now," he said lightly. "Three is the correct number for that sort of thing, isn't it?"

Mrs. Grier seemed struck by the remark.

"There may be something in that, sir," she allowed.

Then one or two others of the head servants, who, having endured the twenty-five years of semi-starvation of the old Squire's rule, had come to be looked upon as fixtures in the place, were in turn introduced by name to Mrs. Chancellor.

"Some of the new servants are to be here to-morrow," said Mrs. Grier, to Captain Chancellor. "I hope you will find everything comfortable in the meantime, sir."

Dinner—or, more properly speaking, supper—was prepared for the travellers in the dining-room—a huge, dark cavern of a room it looked to Eugenia, who shivered as the fireless grate met her view. She was too tired to eat; but, afraid of annoying her husband, she made a pretence of doing so, feeling eager for Sydney's letter, and a chat with Rachel about "home," in her own room.

These pleasures were deferred for a little by the appearance of Mrs. Grier to do the honour of showing her lady her rooms. The housekeeper had rather taken a fancy to Mrs. Chancellor. Eugenia's allusion to what she "must have had to go through," had been a most lucky one, for Mrs. Grier was one of those curiously constituted beings to whom condolence never comes amiss. The most delicate flattery was less acceptable to her than a sympathising remark that she was "looking far from well," and no one could pay her a higher compliment than by telling her she bore traces of having known a great deal of trouble. She was not, for her class, an uneducated person; but she was constitutionally superstitious. Omens, dreams, deathbeds, funerals, all things ghastly and ghostly, were dear to her soul; and her thirty-three years' life in a gloomy, half-deserted house, such as Halswood had been under the old *régime*, had not conduced to a healthier tone of mind.

"Along this way, if you please, ma'am," she said to Eugenia, pointing to the long corridor which ran to the right of the great staircase they had come up by. "The rooms to the left have not been occupied for many years. We thought—that is, Mr. Blinkhorn and I—that you would prefer to use the rooms which have been the best family-rooms for some generations. It would feel less strange-like—more at home, if I may say so. Here, ma'am," opening the first door she came to, "is what was the late Mrs. Chancellor's boudoir. It is eight-and-twenty years next month since she was taken ill suddenly, sitting over there by the window in that very chair. It was heart-disease, I believe. She had had a good deal of trouble in her time, poor lady, for the old Squire was always peculiar. They carried her—*we* did (I was her maid then)—into her bedroom—the next room, ma'am—this," again opening a door, with an air of peculiar gratification in what she was going to say, "and she died the same night in the bed you see, standing as it does now."

The present Mrs. Chancellor gave a little shiver.

"The next room again, ma'am," proceeded Mrs. Grier, "is quite as pleasant a one as this, and about the same size. It is the room in which old Mr. Chancellor breathed his last, last December. He was eighty-nine, ma'am; but he died very hard, for all that. We prepared both these rooms that you might take your choice."

"Thank you," replied Eugenia. "I certainly do not feel as if I preferred either. What rooms did the last Mr. and Mrs. Chancellor use when they were here?" she went on to ask, in a desperate hope that she might light upon some more inviting habitation than these great, dark, musty apartments, with their funereal four-post bedsteads and gloomy associations.

"They had rooms on the other side of the passage," said Mrs. Grier. "Mrs. Chancellor had a prejudice against those *beautiful* mahogany bedsteads," with indignant emphasis. Evidently Herbert Chancellor's wife had found small favour in the eyes of Mrs. Grier. "But Mr. Chancellor *died*," with satisfaction, "in his grandfather's room—the next door, as I told you, ma'am, to this."

"I don't wonder at it," thought Eugenia

to herself. She wished she could find courage to ask if it would not be possible for her at once to take up her quarters in one of the rooms in which, so far at least, no Chancellor had lain in state, and was just meditating a request to be shown the one in which Herbert had *not* died, when Mrs. Grier nipped her hopes in the bud.

"To-morrow, of course, any room can be prepared that you like, ma'am," said the housekeeper; "but for to-night, these two beds are the only ones with sheets on."

There was a slightly aggrieved tone in her voice. Eugenia instantly took alarm that she might have hurt the old lady's feelings.

"Oh, thank you, Mrs. Grier!" she exclaimed. "I am quite satisfied with this room, and I am sure it will be very comfortable. To-morrow I should like you to show me all over the house. Of course I don't yet know how we shall settle about any of the rooms permanently. It depends on Captain Chancellor. He intends to refurnish several. But now I think I will go to bed, if you will send Rachel. I am so tired!"

"You *do* look tired, ma'am. It quite gave me a turn to see you so white when you came first, ma'am," said Mrs. Grier, more cheerfully than she had yet spoken.

And at supper in her own room, when she went downstairs, she confided to Mr. Blinkhorn certain agreeable presentiments with regard to their new mistress.

"A nice-spoken young lady. None of your dressed-up fine ladies like the last Mrs. Chancellor and her daughter, who must have French beds to sleep in, and could never so much as remember one's name. Oh, no, *this* Mrs. Chancellor is a different kind altogether. But, mark my words, Mr. Blinkhorn, she isn't long for this world. The Captain may talk of luck turning—ah, indeed!—was it for nothing I dreamt I saw our new lady with black hair instead of brown? Was it for nothing the looking-glass slipped out of my hands when I was dusting her room again this afternoon?"

"But it didn't break," objected Mr. Blinkhorn.

"Break, what has that to do with it?" exclaimed Mrs. Grier, indignantly. "But I know of old it's no use wasting words on some subjects on you, Mr. Blinkhorn. Those that won't see won't see, but some day you may remember my words."

But, notwithstanding Mrs. Grier's forebodings, notwithstanding her own wounded and troubled spirit, Eugenia Chancellor soon fell asleep, and slept soundly. She fell asleep with Sydney's letter under her pillow, and its loving words in her heart; and the next morning, when the sun shone again, and her husband spoke kindly and seemed to have forgotten yesterday's cloud, she began again to think that after all life might be bright for her, and their home a happy one.

"Comme on pense à vingt ans."

CHAPTER III.

VISITORS, EXPECTED AND UNEXPECTED.

Eins ist was besänftigt; die Liebe.—BÖRNE

YES, things certainly looked brighter next morning, but the brightness was somewhat fitful and tremulous. Encouraged by it, nevertheless, Eugenia made many new resolutions—too many perhaps—and cherished again new hopes. She set herself with palpitating earnestness to please her husband, and repeated to herself, whenever she had reason to think she had done so, that her former failures had been entirely attributable to her own bad management, want of tact, or exaggerated sensitiveness. Her desire to bring herself, and not Captain Chancellor, in guilty; her determination to see him, and everything about him, by the light of her former hopes and beliefs would have been piteous to any one well acquainted with both characters. She was fighting, not merely for happiness, but for faith—her terror, fast maturing, though as yet resolutely ignored, was not so much that her married life should prove a disappointment as that she should be forced into acknowledging the unworthiness of her idol—that the day should come when, in unutterable bitterness of spirit, she should be driven to confess, "behold it was a dream;" when, the glamour gone for ever, the prize she had won should be seen by her for but "a poor thing" after all. For should that day ever come, Eugenia, little as she knew herself, yet felt instinctively it would go sorely with her—ever prone to extremes, her judgment would then be warped by disappointment, as formerly by unreasonable expectation.

"If I ever come to believe Beauchamp selfish, small-minded, or in any sense less noble than my ideal husband," she had once said to herself, "I cannot imagine that I could endure to remain with him—I cannot imagine that I could live. Only," she added, and this reflection many a time stood her in good stead, giving her a sense of security—of firm ground in one direction, "there is one thing I can *never* be disappointed in—the certainty of his love. Even should it die out altogether—should he live to regret his marriage, and think it a mistake, I shall know that it *was* mine—that to win me he threw every other consideration aside."

But just at this time—their first coming to Halswood—Mrs. Chancellor instinctively shunned meditation, and for a while the plan seemed to answer. There was a good deal to do—a good many arrangements to make as to which it was almost a matter of necessity that her husband should consult her. There was all the new furniture to select, the choice of rooms to make, and into these interests Eugenia threw herself with a good deal of her old energy, tempered however by her determination in all things great and small to submit to Beauchamp's wishes—to accept his opinion as incontestably best. And up to a certain point this plan succeeded, and, difficult as it was for Eugenia to live in a state of semi-suppression, of incessant watchfulness over each word, and tone, and even look for fear that in any way she should offend, yet she fancied she believed she was doing no more than her wifely duty—that she was happy in acting thus, and that by-and-by, "when we get to understand each other," life would be all she had dreamed of.

But to an essentially honest nature this self-delusion could not be kept up for ever. Nor, notwithstanding all the goodwill in the world, was it possible for Eugenia—impulsive, vehement, yearning for sympathy, and eager to confide to the friend nearest to her every thought, doubt, hope which sprang to life in her busy brain—for long to adhere to the rule of conduct she had laid down for herself. Her very conscientiousness, her very humility ranged themselves against her; how could she judge or interpret the conduct or opinions of the man she would have gladly died rather than lose her lofty faith in, by a standard lower than that by which she tested herself? She never yet had allowed to herself the existence of the creeping, encroaching, serpent-like fear she dared not face; but, nevertheless, it was making its way to the very centre of her fortress. Day by day she propped up its tottering foundations with some feeble, inefficient attempt at a bulwark—some plausible excuse or suggestion of misapprehension or undeserved self-blame—refusing to see how the whole once beautiful fabric was doomed, how the best remaining chance for her was bravely to make an end of it, to set to work again with the materials yet left to her to uprear a less imposing but more firmly-built tower of defence, better fitted than her fairy palace to stand, not only the great storms, but the smaller trials —the daily damps, and mists, and chills of life.

But this, Eugenia would not do. She clung with desperate infatuation to her dream, and in her heart of hearts she said—

"If it is to end in ruin, let it be so, and

great will be the fall thereof. But I will not hasten my own misery by thinking about it beforehand."

They had been now between two and three months at Halswood; the weeks had at the very first passed quickly enough, for Eugenia had succeeded in filling them with a succession of petty interests. Captain Chancellor was very well pleased with her, on the whole. She had proved more submissive than he had anticipated, though a great part of the credit of this satisfactory state of things was doubtless due to his own judicious management. He had always had his own theories as to the proper way of controlling and training the opposite sex, and had often been contemptuous on the subject of unhappy marriages.

"Unhappy fiddlesticks," he would declare, "it's all his own fault. He should have given her to understand once for all at the start who was to be master, and he would have had no more trouble."

The trouble that had fallen to his own share he owned to himself had certainly not been great, and the proof of the pudding being generally allowed to be in the eating, he felt pleasantly conscious of his own success. There was only one thing about his wife that ever seriously annoyed him—her spirits were not of late what they had been; certainly, some amount of repose and reserve of manner had been wanting in her at first, and he was pleased to see how quickly she had, at a hint or two from him, set herself to acquire it; but then, again, there had been a great charm in her girlish gaiety and graceful merriment.

"I never heard any woman laugh better than Eugenia," he thought. "Most women laugh so atrociously, that I wish it was made penal, but she laughs charmingly."

Then he wondered why of late he had so seldom heard that sweet, soft, bright sound. "She can't be dull," he said to himself, "we have had a fair amount of variety since we came here. Besides, catch a woman being dull and not complaining of it! And if there is anything she wants, she would have been sure to ask for it."

He firmly believed himself the most indulgent of husbands, and so, in a certain practical sense, perhaps he was. He "grudged her nothing," though, indeed, her tastes continued so simple, that her own allowance from her father promised more than to cover her whole personal expenses; he never went away from home without bringing her some costly present when he came back—the first time, it had been a bracelet of great value. Eugenia had thanked him for it warmly, but then, eyeing it with some misgiving, had said something about its being too good for her.

"I don't feel as if I liked wearing such splendid things, Beauchamp," had been her words. "It hardly seems consistent with ——"

"With what?" he had asked, irritated already.

"With my former quiet life, with present things, even, my sister being the wife of a poor curate, for one thing. But oh, don't be vexed, Beauchamp, I am very silly, I know. Forgive me. For the *thought* of me, the wish to please me, I cannot thank you enough. That would have delighted me had the bracelet been the plainest in the world."

Upon which, Beauchamp had turned from her angrily, with some muttered words about "sentimental nonsense and affectation," and Eugenia had had a sore fit of penitence for the inexcusable ingratitude which had thus wounded his sensitive spirit. And, after all, she did deserve some blame for unnecessarily irritating him in this instance.

And thus, whether really the case or not, it always seemed to him in any of the discussions or disagreements which still, notwithstanding Eugenia's scrupulous care, occasionally arose between them. And no wonder that he thought so. It was always the same story. Eugenia annoyed him, probably in some very trivial matter, as to which, nevertheless, he felt bound to act up to his principle of "keeping a tight hand on her, letting her feel the reins."

And invariably it ended in her taking all the blame on herself, exerting all her powers of logic (or sophistry) to convince herself that the fault lay with her alone. It was but rarely, very, very rarely, that she allowed her strong true sense of justice, of self-respect and womanly right, to break out from the restraint in which she had condemned it to dwell. And on such occasions, according to the invariable law of reaction, the unnatural repression avenged itself, and as had been the case in the carriage the night they came to Halswood, Eugenia's bitterness of indignation and fiery temper horrified herself, and did her infinite injustice with her husband. It was a bad state of things altogether—bad for Eugenia, worse, perhaps, for her husband, fostering his selfishness, increasing his narrow-minded self-opinionativeness.

The day after the one on which it had occurred to Beauchamp that Eugenia's spirits were not what they had been, it happened that she got a letter from Sydney. It came in the morning, and as Captain

Chancellor handed it to her, a joyful exclamation escaped her.

"From Sydney! Oh, I am so glad! I have not heard from her for such a time."

"What do you call 'such a time,' I wonder?" said Captain Chancellor, good-humouredly. "A week, I suppose?"

"No, longer than that," replied Eugenia. And then, encouraged by his tone, she added, "You know Sydney and I had hardly ever been separated before, and lately I have been particularly anxious to hear from home —from Wareborough—on account of my father not having been well."

"Your father ill! I never heard of it. I wonder you did not tell me," said her husband.

"It was when you were away—the week before last—I heard it. I think I mentioned it when I wrote," said Eugenia, timidly, reluctant to own to herself that Beauchamp could so soon have forgotten a matter of such interest to her.

"Ah, well, perhaps you did. It is nothing serious, I suppose?" And without waiting for an answer, Captain Chancellor proceeded to read his own letters.

One among them was from an old brother officer, a friend of several years' standing, recently returned from abroad, whom he had invited to come down for a few days' shooting, intending to arrange a suitable party to meet him.

"Eugenia," he said, looking up quickly, after reading this letter, "Colonel Masterton cannot come till the 29th. That leaves us all the week after next free. Of course I shall not ask the others till he comes. How would you like to have your people for a few days then—the Thurstons and your father. The change might do him good, and you seem dying to see your sister."

Eugenia's face glowed all over with delight. The old bright look came into her eyes, the old eager ring thrilled again through her voice.

"Oh, Beauchamp, thank you, thank you so much for thinking of it. It would be delightful. I cannot tell you how I should enjoy it."

"Why have you never spoken of it before if you wish it so much?" asked Beauchamp, not unkindly, but with the slight irritation of incipient self-reproach. "I can't *guess* your wishes always, you know."

"I did mention it once," she said, timidly again. "Don't you remember, the first time you had to go away I asked if Sydney might come to me."

"But that was an absurd proposal. It would have looked so ridiculous to bring Mrs. Thurston all the way here because I was to be away, and naturally when your friends do come I should wish to be at home to receive them; so you had better write about their coming, to-day."

He rose as he spoke, and gathering his letters and newspapers together, left the room, feeling very well pleased with himself, and not sorry to see the bright flush of happiness his proposal had brought to his wife's pale cheeks.

She was indeed feeling very happy. Never since her marriage, since at least the first few days of unalloyed enjoyment in

Paris—had she felt so eagerly delighted about anything. And the bright gleam had not come before it was wanted. Notwithstanding Beauchamp's comfortable belief that they had had a fair amount of variety since coming to Halswood, Eugenia's life had latterly been very dull. The most pleasurable part of the variety had fallen to his own share—two or three "runs up to town" to see about the new furniture, or new carriages, or something of the kind; one or two short visits to bachelor shooting-boxes, to which ladies were not invited; plenty of the exhilarating out-door life, which he thoroughly enjoyed, to which as yet Eugenia, not over strong, and completely unaccustomed to horses, was not sufficiently acclimatised to find it enjoyable. No wonder Captain Chancellor considered that the last three months had been far from dull. They would not have seemed so to Eugenia, had her inner life been a more natural and healthy one; but as it was, the outside distractions that had come in her way had been few and by no means powerful.

Most of the "families of position" in the neighbourhood had called on them, but the very biggest people of all—a family residing at a considerable distance from Halswood—had not yet done so; and Beauchamp's evident anxiety on this point had not been unobserved by Eugenia, though resolutely put aside by her as one of the things into which she would not look. Some of their neighbours had already invited them to dinner, and they had gone; but Eugenia had not enjoyed the experience, and felt little wish to renew it. "Long ago," as now in her own mind she had learnt to call her girlhood, even the dullest of dinner-parties would have furnished her quick observation, her lively imagination, her fresh, eager nature with material for interest and entertainment. But now-a-days it was different. She was self-conscious and self-absorbed, and, as a matter of course, less attractive in herself, less ready to find others so. Her one engrossing sensation in company was anxiety to please, or at least to avoid displeasing her husband, which left her none of the leisure of mind or self-forgetfulness essential to her enjoyment of the people or scenes about her. And these had not been sufficiently striking or interesting to force her out of herself. There were not many young people in the neighbourhood; those of her own sex nearest in age to Eugenia happening at this time to be either young girls not yet out of the schoolroom, or youthful matrons, with whom Mrs. Chancellor could not feel that she had much in common. They all seemed happy and busy, perfectly at ease, satisfied with their lives and themselves. "Or else," thought Eugenia, "they are more clever at hiding their anxieties and disappointments than I am." In many cases doubtless true. She had not yet learnt, as most women of deep feeling sooner or later must learn, to smile when the heart feels all but breaking, to force interest in the trivialities around one, when one's own life, or what may be dearer than life, seems hanging in the balance. At this stage of her history, such seeming she would probably have stigmatized as mere hypocrisy, not taking into account that unselfishness and worthy self-respect, as often as pride, furnish the motive for the wearing of that most tragic "des masques tragiques—celui qui avait un sourire."

So, though her beauty and gentleness prepossessed many in her favour—many even of those whose prejudices as well as curiosity had been aroused by the fact that the wife of the new master of Halswood was not exactly of their world, belonging, indeed, to one of "those dreadful manufacturing places, where the sun never shines for the smoke, and all the people drop their *h*'s, you know" —Eugenia Chancellor did not make much way among her new acquaintances. The women allowed she was "pretty" and unassuming, but stupid or shy, they were not sure which. The men hooted at "pretty"— "lovely" or "beautiful" was nearer the mark—and hesitated about the "shy or stupid" suggestion, coming, however, in almost every case to allow that she was difficult to get on with—either "Chancellor bullied her at home," or she had married him without caring for him; that she was not happy was evident. At which proof of masculine discrimination, the wives and mothers held up their hands in scornful incredulity. It was "just like Fred, or Arthur, or 'your papa,' to make a romantic mystery about her, because she is pretty. There is nothing plainer to see than that she is silent and stiff because she feels rather out of her element as yet. It is all strange to her, of course, having been brought up as she has been, and really she is to be felt for."

But the "feeling for her," giving itself vent in one or two instances in the direction of a disposition to patronize, was not responded to; and after a while the temporary sensation on the subject of Mrs. Chancellor died away, especially when it oozed out that Lady Hereward had not yet called at Halswood.

Little cared Eugenia, as she ran upstairs to consult her lugubrious friend Mrs. Grier on the subject of the prettiest and pleasantest rooms to be forthwith—fifteen days beforehand—prepared for her expected guests.

"My sister, Mrs. Thurston, and my father, are coming the week after next," she announced to the housekeeper, ignoring the possibility of the yet un-posted letter of invitation receiving any but a favourable reply. "You must let me know if you think of *anything* wanting for these rooms."

And the bright expectation in the young face touched even Mrs. Grier's unready sympathy in joy. She forgave Eugenia's presumptuous rejection of the gloomy chambers, long since deserted in favour of more cheerful quarters, by the master and mistress of the house, where the funereal four-posters still reigned, and was inspired to suggest ever so many tiny wants and improvements which sent her young mistress off to Chilworth in the brougham, in a pleasant excitement of novel housewifely importance. It was but seldom that interests of the kind offered themselves to Eugenia— another of the unfortunate blanks in her new life—for Mrs. Grier, notwithstanding her dreams and visions, was, practically, an excellent head of affairs. Everything about the house was always in perfect order. If the under-servants proved inefficient or otherwise undesirable they were sent away, and Mrs. Grier or Blinkhorn procured others; if the dinner was not thoroughly to Captain Chancellor's liking, one or other of this responsible pair was informed of the fact, and desired to see it remedied, or, in a case of unusual gravity, the "chef" himself would be summoned to receive personal instruction from his master, who considered himself, and very probably justly, no mean authority on gastronomical problems.

"There is really very little for me to do," wrote Eugenia once to her sister. "Beauchamp does not care for me to meddle in the housekeeping, and I can see it is far better done than it would be by me. All the new furniture has come, and of course it is beautiful. I took a good deal of interest in choosing it, but it isn't half such fun as when one has to think how one can make one's money get all one wants. And I think the rooms are too big to enjoy the prettiness of the things. Do you remember the choosing of your drawing-room carpet? I am afraid, Sydney dear, I am quite out of my element as a fine lady. There are no poor people, even, that I can hear of. They all seem dreadfully well off, and well looked after by the clergyman and the agent and their wives. I wish I could study more, but I think I have got lazy, or else it is the difference of having to do everything alone. There are lots of books in the library—many whose names even I never heard. I wish I had papa's direction! We get all our new books from town once a month, but they very seldom send the ones I want, and when they do I want you to talk them over with."

Sydney sighed as she read this letter. It was not often Eugenia wrote so despondently, but Sydney's perceptions were acute.

"Poor Eugenia," she thought. "It isn't only these outside things which are wrong, I fear. If other things had equalled her hopes, these would have been all right. The want lies deeper, I fear—the blank is one hard to fill. How I wish I could see her!"

The next week brought Eugenia's invitation. It would have been difficult to decline it. "You *must* come," she wrote. "I am living in the thoughts of it, Sydney; it will be absolute cruelty to refuse. I cannot tell you how I long to see you all again."

So, though leaving home even for a few days, was now no small effort to Mr. Laurence, and though Frank Thurston groaned a good deal in anticipation, he "hated fine houses and grand people," and all *his* people, the East-enders of Wareborough, would go to the bad in double-quick time if he let them out of his sight for the best part of a week; who would take the night schools? who would see to the confirmation classes? &c. &c. &c.—it ended, as Sydney had quietly determined it should, in a letter of acceptance being sent to Halswood by return of post. And Mrs. Thurston took the opportunity of chaffing her husband a little on what she termed his growing self-conceit.

"'Un bon prêtre,'" she said, "'c'est bien bon.' I quite agree with Jean Valjean. But still, Frank, of the very best of things it is possible to have too much."

Whereupon Frank told her she was very impertinent. There was little fear of these two misunderstanding each other.

There is a mischievous French proverb which tells us that "le malheur n'est jamais si près de nous qu'alors que tout nous sourit." Things were certainly *more* smiling than usual with Eugenia Chancellor the morning that she received Sydney's cheerful acceptance of the invitation to Halswood, and was graciously told by Beauchamp in answer to her announcement of the news "that he was glad they were coming, and he hoped the weather would be fine." But misfortune—disappointment, at least, was near at hand; misfortune in the shape of a plain-looking little old lady in a shabby pony carriage, who about an hour after luncheon this same day made her appearance under the ugly portico, and learning that Mrs. Chancellor was at home, alighted, and was shown into the morning-room, giving a name for announcement to the footman newly imported from town, which, taken in conjunction with her unimposing appearance, somewhat excited that gentleman's surprise.

She had not driven in by the grand entrance, but by the second best lodge, that on the road leading to the village of Stebbing-le-Bray. Captain Chancellor, setting off on a long ride, passed the old lady in the funny little carriage, and, wondering who she could be, asked for information on the subject from the man at the lodge, a venerable person thoroughly up in local celebrities. The answer he received caused him to open his handsome blue eyes, and to change his programme for the afternoon. He rode out at the Stebbing lodge, made a cut across the country which brought him on to the Chilworth Road, and re-entering his own domain, dismounted at home twenty minutes after he had set off, to find his wife and the little old lady in evidently friendly converse in the morning room.

Somewhat startled by her husband's unlooked-for reappearance, uncertain if he and her visitor were already acquainted, Eugenia hesitated a moment in introducing her companions. But the stranger was quite equal to the occasion.

"How do you do, Captain Chancellor?" she said, cordially. "I am so pleased to meet you at last. By *hearsay*, do you know, you are already an old friend of mine?"

Beauchamp bowed with a slight air of inquiry.

"A nephew of mine, or, to be exact, which they say women never are, a grand-nephew of my husband's, has so often spoken of you to me. You will remember him—George Vandeleur; he was in your regiment in the Crimea, though you have seldom met each other since?"

Captain Chancellor's face lightened up, and what Eugenia called his nicest look came over it. He had been very kind to young Vandeleur, at the time little more than a boy, and it was pleasant to find himself remembered.

Lady Hereward had the happiest knack of saying agreeable things, of pleasing when she wished to please. Those who liked her liked her thoroughly, and trusted her implicitly; but, on the other hand, those who disliked her were quite as much in earnest about it. And both parties, I suspect, coalesced in being more or less afraid of her, for, insignificant as she appeared, she could hit hard in certain directions, though her heart was true, her sympathies wide. Coming, perhaps, within Roma Eyrecourt's category of "those to whom it was easy to be good," there had certainly been nothing in the circumstances of her life to develop meanness in any form, and on this, in whatever guise she came across it—humbug, petty ambition, class prejudice—she was therefore, as is the tendency of poor humanity towards the foibles oneself "is not inclined to," apt to be rather too hard. Since birth she had been placed in a perfectly assured and universally recognised position. She had had nothing to be ambitious about; even her want of beauty had not amounted to a trial, for her powers of fascination, as is sometimes the case with plain women, had been more than compensatingly great; and before she was twenty she had had every unexceptionable *parti* of the day at her feet. How it came to pass she was not "spoilt" those who knew her best often marvelled, but even they did not know all about her. For she had had her sorrows, had passed through a fiery furnace—how it all happened matters little, the love-story of a plain-looking old woman of sixty would hardly be interesting begun at the wrong end—and the gold of her nature had emerged, therefrom, unwasted and pure. In the end she had married, at twenty-two, Lord Hereward, a peer of great wealth and position, a man whom she liked and respected, and with whom she had bravely made the best of her life. Trouble was not over for her yet, however. She had two children, a son who grew up satisfactorily to man's estate, behaving himself creditably at school, and college, and everywhere, who in time married, as was to be expected, and became the centre of another family; and a daughter, who was as the apple of her mother's eye, whom she loved as strong natures only can love. And one day—one awful day—the little daughter died suddenly and painfully, and Margaret Hereward's heart broke.

And all the outside world said: "How sad for the poor Herewards; but what a blessing it was not the boy," and then forgot all about it, for the chief sufferer never reminded any one of her woe.

It was forty years ago now, and few remembered that a little Lady Alice Godwin had ever existed. In time, of course, her mother came to learn that even with a broken heart one can go on living, and her healthy nature reasserted itself in an increased power of sympathy—an active energy in lightening or, at least, sharing other women's sorrows. But still, as she grew older, she hardened in her special dislikes, her pet intolerances.

She went on talking about her nephew for a while, explaining, by the way, how it was she had come to make her first call at Halswood in so informal a fashion.

"I am staying at Stebbing Rectory for a day or two," she said. "A young cousin of mine is the wife of Mr. Mervyn, the clergyman there. She has just got her first baby—a little girl;" she paused for an instant; "such a nice baby, and I came over to look after her a little. She has no mother. Hearing how very near I was to you, I thought I would not miss the opportunity of seeing you so easily. It is a long drive from Marshlands here. When you come to see me it must not be only for a call."

She did not tell that the calling on the new Mrs. Chancellor, which had been a vague and indefinite intention in her mind before coming to Stebbing, had taken active form, from hearing from her cousin some of the local gossip about the stranger—that she was pretty, but so stiff and reserved that no one could get on with her; that some people called her awkward and underbred, others suspected that she was not happy

(Mrs. Mervyn's own opinion), but that from one cause or another her life bid fair to become a lonely and isolated one. And the sight of Eugenia's face rewarded the old lady for the kindly effort she had made. It was not so much her beauty, though Lady Hereward loved to see a pretty face; it was her sweet, bright, yet wistful expression, that straightway touched the maternal chord in her visitor's heart. Possibly, too, contradiction had something to do with the interest Eugenia at once awakened.

"Underbred, indeed!" she said to herself, contemptuously. "I wish I could teach some people I know, what good breeding really is. As to her being unhappy, I can't say. I must see more of her."

She acted at once on this determination, for, before she left, she invited her new young friends to spend three days of the next week but one at Marshlands. There was a particular reason for fixing this time; "George" was coming, and would be delighted to meet Captain Chancellor again.

"I would give you a choice if I could," she went on, fancying that she perceived a slight hesitation in Mrs. Chancellor's manner, "for I really do want you to come. But I fear I cannot. We are going away the end of the same week to Hereward, for some time. We old people need a breath of sea air now and then."

"It is exceedingly kind of you. I should have liked *very* much to go to you the week after next," began Eugenia, looking as if she meant what she said. "It is so unlucky—but I am afraid we must decline. We are engaged for the whole of that week at home. You remember, Beauchamp? I heard this morning that——"

"I think you have made a confusion between the week after next and the week after *that*," said Captain Chancellor, blandly. "I don't know of anything to prevent our accepting Lady Hereward's invitation. We did expect some friends; but, don't you remember, Eugenia, that Colonel Masterton put off his visit for a week?"

"Yes," said Eugenia, quietly; "I remember."

"Then may I hope to see you," asked Lady Hereward, feeling a little puzzled, "on Tuesday?—that will be the 22nd. George comes the same day."

"Certainly," said Beauchamp. "We shall be delighted to join you."

And "Thank you—you are very, very kind," said Eugenia again.

The tone in which the simple words were uttered was almost girlishly cordial, yet, somehow, Lady Hereward did not feel satisfied. "Her manner *is* a little peculiar," she thought to herself, as she drove back again to Stebbing-le-Bray, "though at first she seemed so frank. I hope my invitation did not really interfere with anything. Could it be shyness that made her not want to come? How very lovely her eyes are! I wonder if my Alice's eyes would have looked like that—they were brown. Alice would not have been so pretty. And, dear me, by this time she might have had a daughter as old as that child! Ah, my little Alice!"

When Lady Hereward had gone, Eugenia

sat still for a moment or two, then rose and left the room. In the hall she met her husband.

"Where are you going?" he said. "Come in here for a minute," opening the door of his study, beside which they were standing. She followed him, but did not sit down. "Tell me," he went on, "how do you like the old lady?"

"Very much," replied Eugenia; then turned again, as if eager to go.

"What are you in such a hurry about? Can't you wait a minute?" he said, impatiently. "Where are you going?"

"To write to Sydney, of course, to put off their visit," she answered, her lips quivering. "I must do it at once."

"Confound Sydney!" he broke out, rudely. "Your temper, Eugenia, is enough to provoke a saint. Wait an instant—do be reasonable—why can't you propose to Sydney to——"

But he had gone too far. Eugenia turned and looked at him for a moment with the unlovely light of angry indignation in her eyes; then left the room quietly.

"By Jove!" said Beauchamp, when left to himself, "I begin to suspect I have been a great fool, after all!"

But reflection and a cigar soothed him a little; half an hour later he followed his wife to her boudoir. She was writing busily.

"Eugenia," he began, "I am sorry for my rudeness just now, but you are very unreasonable. Why can't you write to your people, and ask them to come on the Friday? We return then. Any one but you would understand my reasons for wishing to go to Marshlands."

"I do understand them, rather too well," replied his wife, coldly. "As for asking my people to come on Friday, it is out of the question. My brother-in-law cannot be away on Sunday; and besides, I cannot ask my father and Sydney—neither of them strong—to come so long a journey for only two days."

"Why for only two days?"

"Because on Monday all *your* friends are

coming, and you do not wish mine to be here at the same time."

"I never said anything of the kind," exclaimed Beauchamp, angrily, aware nevertheless that he had *thought* something very much of the kind. It was not that he was ashamed of Mr. Laurence or Sydney; he liked them both very well; but there had been a good deal of "chaff" about his Wareborough marriage, and he had imagined more. He could ill bear chaff, and his constitutional and avowed arrogance laid him peculiarly open to it in certain directions. How he had sneered and made fun of other men in the old days for being "caught" by a pretty face or a pair of bright eyes! He was not ashamed of his marriage—he was proud of his wife in herself—but on the whole, he preferred that his old friends, on their first visit, should not find the house full of his Wareborough relations-in-law. But he had not imagined that Eugenia suspected this.

"I never said anything of the kind," he repeated, working himself into a rage. "But

I warn you, Eugenia, if you don't take care what you are about, you will drive me into thinking, and saying too, many things I never wish to think or say."

She got up from her seat, and stood facing him.

"I know what you mean," she said, huskily, a white despair creeping over her face. "You mean that you regret your marriage. Why did you do it at all then?—tell me. Why did you make me think you everything great and noble, to open my eyes now like this? Why did you not leave me where I was, happy and loved, instead of making me care for you? Why did you ask me to be your wife?"

"Why, indeed? You may well ask," replied Captain Chancellor, in a bitter, contemptuous tone.

Then he turned and left the room. He put down all she had said to "temper," of course; but some of her words had wounded and mortified him not a little.

Eugenia stood there where he had left her, in blank, bewildered misery. Only one thought glanced with any brightness through the black cloud of wretchedness which seemed to choke her.

"He did love me once," she said to herself. "If all the rest was a dream, still he did love me once."

And but for this, she thought she *must* have died.

CHAPTER IV.

"BY THE SPRING."

Life, that dares send
A challenge to his end,
And when it comes, say, "Welcome, friend."
                          CRASHAW.

TUESDAY the 22nd came, but Captain Chancellor set off on his visit to Marshlands alone. Eugenia was ill—too ill to leave her room, though better than she had been. The restrained suffering of the last few weeks, the unhealthily reserved and isolated life she had begun to live—she to whom sympathy was as the air she breathed—all had told upon her; and the excitement of the painful discussion with her husband the day of Lady Hereward's unfortunate visit, had been the finishing-stroke. After that she gave way altogether.

She was not sorry to be ill. On the whole, she felt it the best thing that could have happened to her. She was glad to be alone.

She was very glad now that Sydney's visit had been deferred. With all her haste and impulsiveness, there was in her a curious mixture of clear-headedness and reasoning power. She liked to understand things—to get to the bottom of them. Now that she had left off pretending to deceive herself with false representations—now that she had ceased to try to cheat herself into imagining she was happy—she found a strange, half-morbid satisfaction in dissecting and analysing the whole—her own character and her husband's; the past lives of both, and the influences that had made them what they were; the special, definite causes of their discordancy.

"He is not—I see it plainly now," she said to herself, with a curious, hopeless sort of calm, "he is not in the very least the man I imagined. *That* Beauchamp has never existed. Is it just, therefore, that I should blame the real one for not being what he never was?" Here she got a little puzzled, and tried to look at it from a fresh point of view. "And being what he is, and no more, why should I not make the best of it? It seems to me there is something repulsive and unworthy in the thought. I would almost rather go on being miserable. Yet I suppose many women have had to do it. I could fancy Sydney, for instance, doing it, and never letting any one suspect she had had it to do. In time, perhaps, I may find it easier, or grow callous."

Then she would set to work to think out a new rôle for herself—that of an utterly lonely, impossibly self-reliant woman, living a life of self-abnegation, of lofty devotion to duty—unappreciated devotion, unsuspected abnegation—such as no woman has ever yet lived since women were. Seen through the softening medium of physical weakness, not amounting to actual suffering, this new way of looking at things came to have a certain attraction for her. The idea of total and lasting sacrifice of all hopes of personal happiness, all yearning for sympathy, was grand enough and impossible enough to recommend itself greatly to this ardent, extreme nature, to which anything was better than second bests, nothing so antagonistic as compromise in any form.

"I have staked my all and lost," she said to herself with a sort of piteous grandiloquence; "there is nothing left me but duty and endurance; for though he *did* love me, I doubt if he does so now. I am not necessary to his happiness. He does not and cannot understand me."

Only unfortunately there were two or three little difficulties in the way of settling down comfortably to this conclusion. In the first place, notwithstanding her love of theorizing, and of idealizing even the woes of her lot, Eugenia was essentially honest, and being so she could not allow to herself that her conduct had been blameless, especially in this last and most serious disagreement. She had said things which she knew would gall and irritate her husband. In the morbid excitement of the moment she owned to herself that she had even wished them to have this effect, that his behaviour might excuse the violence of her indignation. And her conduct in general—her conduct ever since their marriage—ever since, at least, the first few weeks of careless happiness— how did that now appear to her from her new point of view? She knew she had been gentle, and in a superficial sense unselfish; with but very rare exceptions she had entirely merged her own wishes in those of her husband, had opposed nothing that he had suggested. Such submission, such sinking of her own individuality, had been unnatural and forced, completely foreign to her character. And what had been its motive? Not the highest—far from it. It had not been that she really believed that in so doing she was acting her wifely part to perfection; it had not been earnest endeavour after the best within her reach that had prompted her, but rather, a cowardly, a selfish determination to close her eyes to the facts of her life—a weak refusal to see anything she did not want to see—the old wilful cry, "All or nothing; give me all or I die"—the shrinking from owning, even to herself, the self-willed impetuosity with which she had acted—the terror of acknowledging that she had been deceived, or rather, had deceived herself.

"Yes," she said, "I have been all wrong

together. How selfish I have been too! Months ago how indignant I used to get with poor Sydney if she ever attempted, as she used to call it, to 'clip my wings for me.' How angry I was with papa when he suggested that we should defer our marriage till we knew a little more of each other! How selfish I was in Paris, too—selfish and unsympathizing in Beauchamp's change of fortune! Perhaps, after all, it is no more than I have deserved that he should feel as he does now."

The reflection was a wholesome one, and its influence softening, and Beauchamp had been very kind since her illness. He might not understand her, but at times she felt it was certainly going too far to say that he no longer cared for her. He seemed to have already quite forgotten all about this last discussion, and in truth the impression it had made upon him had been by no means a deep one. "It was all a fit of temper of Eugenia's," he said to himself, and as one of his fixed ideas was that such a thing as a woman without a temper had never existed, he resigned himself to his fate, with the hope that his share of this unavoidable drawback to the charms of married life might be small.

Up to the last Captain Chancellor hoped that his wife would be able to accompany him to Marshlands. To do him justice, he was very reluctant to go without her.

"It is such a pity," he said. "It would be just what I should like, for you to see a good deal of Lady Hereward. It isn't every one that she takes to, I can tell you."

"I like her in herself," said Eugenia; "the only thing I dislike her for is that she is Lady Hereward. I got tired of her name before I had ever seen her."

The moment she had said this she regretted it. Beauchamp's brow clouded over.

"Of course," he replied, coldly, "if you set yourself against her I can't help it. Perhaps the best plan would be for me to write making an excuse for us both, and have done with the acquaintance. I am sick of discussions about everything I propose."

It was hard upon her; it was so seldom,

so very seldom she had opposed him in anything, or even expressed an opinion.

"I am very sorry I cannot go," she said, "but your giving up going is not to be thought of. There is no reason for it. I am not seriously ill. There is nothing wrong with me but what a few days' rest will set right."

This was true. So Captain Chancellor set off for Marshlands alone, and Eugenia, solitary and suffering, spent in her own room the week she had so eagerly anticipated.

Time went on. November past, midwinter is soon at hand, and Christmas had come and gone before, contrary to the Chilworth doctor's sanguine opinion, Mrs. Chancellor was at all like herself again. It was a dreary winter to her. Had she been in good health, some reaction from the hopeless depression which had gradually taken hold of her would have been pretty sure to set in—a reaction, perhaps, of a sound and healthy nature; possibly, nevertheless, of the reverse. This, however, was not the case. At the beginning of her illness, things had looked more promising: her husband's kindness had touched and softened her, her own reflections had pointed the right way. But as the days went on and Eugenia felt herself growing weaker instead of stronger, her clearer view of things clouded over again. It takes a great reserve of mutual trust and sympathy to stand the wearing effects of a trying though not acute illness. Beauchamp got tired of his wife's never being well—so at least she fancied—tired of it, and then indifferent, or if not indifferent, accustomed to it. And whether this was really the case or not, there was some excuse for her believing it to be so, for the habitual small selfishness of his nature was thrown out in strong relief by circumstances undoubtedly trying.

"If people looked forward to realities, they would choose their husbands and wives differently. It is only about a year ago since I first met Beauchamp. Oh, how silly and ignorant I must have been!

How perfect life—life with him—looked to me," thought Eugenia, bitterly.

She was more than usually depressed that day. Captain Chancellor had left home to spend a week at Winsley, where a merry Christmas party was expected, and though Eugenia had no wish to accompany him, even had she been able to do so, though she had not put the slightest difficulty in the way of his going, yet his readiness to do so wounded and embittered her. For he had got into the habit of often leaving home now—never for very long at a time, certainly—never without making every arrangement for her comfort; but yet the fact of his liking to go, increased her unhappy state of mind. Everything seemed against her. During all these months she had never succeeded in seeing her own people. Another invitation had been sent to them and accepted. For Eugenia had had the unselfishness to place the deferring of their first visit in a natural and favourable light, making it appear to be quite as much her own doing as her husband's, and a subject of great regret to both.

"Better that they should think I have grown cold and indifferent even," she thought, "than that they should suspect the truth." But no one except Frank had at this time thought anything of the kind.

"*I* wont go, another time," he growled. "I never heard anything so cool in my life. If it is Eugenia's own doing, I don't want to have anything more to say to her. If not, I pity her, but she chose her husband herself."

And Sydney had some difficulty to smooth him down again, and to gain his consent to the acceptance of the second invitation when in course of time it made its appearance.

It was accepted, but the visit did not take place. Before the date fixed for it arrived, Mr. Laurence had another attack of illness, from which he only recovered sufficiently to be moved to a milder place, where for a few weeks, Sydney, though at no small personal inconvenience, accompanied him. Something was said by her in one of her letters to Eugenia, suggestive of her joining them and taking her share in the nursing and cheering of their father; but the proposal met with no response. Loyal and true-hearted as she was, Sydney felt chilled and disappointed, and said no more. But all through the winter, in reality passed by Eugenia in loneliness, and suffering, and yearning for sympathy, which only a mistaken desire to spare her sister sorrow prevented her expressing— all these months Sydney pictured her as happy and prosperous, so free from cares herself as to be in danger of forgetting their existence in the lives of others. For the more steadily hopeless Eugenia grew, the more cheerfully she wrote. And forced cheerfulness often bears a strong resemblance to heartlessness.

"I am glad and thankful she is happy," thought Sydney, "and she certainly must be so, for it is not in her to conceal it if she were not; but I did not think prosperity would have changed Eugenia."

Nor would she, for any conceivable consideration, have owned to any one, least of all perhaps to her husband, that she *did* think so.

Mr. Laurence had fortunately no misgivings on the subject of his elder daughter. She was happy, she wrote regularly and affectionately—she had twice fixed a time for him to visit her, but circumstances had come in the way. It was all quite right. He loved her as fondly as ever, with perhaps a shade *more* fondness than the child "who was ever with him," whose new ties had in no wise been allowed to interfere with her daughterly devotion; it never occurred to him that Eugenia's affection could be dimmed.

"I should like to see her," he said sometimes—"I should like to see her very much—in her own home too. But by the spring we shall be able to arrange for it; by the spring, no doubt, I shall be more like myself again, and able to manage a little going about. We must go together, Sydney, my dear, as Eugenia wished."

And Sydney said, "Yes, by the spring

they must arrange it." But a shadowy misgiving, that had visited her not unfrequently of late—a little, painful, choking feeling in her throat, a sudden moisture in her eyes, made themselves felt, when she looked at her father's thin, worn face, and heard him talk about "the spring;" and she wondered, as so many loving watchers wonder, "if the doctors had told her the whole truth."

There had always been a certain unworldliness about Mr. Laurence—a gentle philosophy, an unexacting unselfishness, and of late all these had increased. Practical as he had proved himself in his far-seeing philanthropy, he was a man to whom it came naturally to live much in the unseen, to whom the thought that "to this life there is a to-morrow," was full of encouragement and consolation—a to-morrow in more senses than the one of individual blessedness—a to-morrow when the work begun here, however poor and imperfect in itself, shall be carried on, purified, strengthened, rendered a thousand times more powerful for good—

a to-morrow even for the races yet unborn in this world. All this he believed, and his life had shown that he did so. Yet many people shook their heads over his "want of religious principle," his "dangerously lax notions," and prophesied that no blessing could follow the labours of such a man. But such sayings little troubled Sydney's father. He smiled with kindly tolerance, and thought to himself that some time or other such things would come to be viewed differently.

About the middle of February, Mr. Laurence and his daughter returned home to Wareborough. On the last day of March, Sydney's boy was born—a strong, handsome, satisfactory baby—with whom the young parents were greatly delighted. Sydney recovered her strength quickly, and before April was over, Mr. Laurence, who had seemed much better of late, and who had taken wonderfully to his grandson, began to talk again of the often-deferred visit to Eugenia.

"It would be a nice little change for you,

Sydney, and Eugenia would be so pleased to see her little nephew. Her letters are full of questions about him. I have a great mind to write to her myself, and ask what time next month would be convenient for her to receive us. I think my doing so would please her. I should be sorry for her to think we had not taken the first opportunity of going to see her. They are sure to be at home next month?"

"Yes," said Sydney, "I remember Eugenia's saying in one of her letters, that they were not going to town this year. I don't know why, for not long ago she said something about their probably buying a house in town. Well, father dear, baby and I — and Frank too, I dare say — will be ready whenever you arrange for it with Eugenia."

But Mr. Laurence never wrote. The very next day—it was early in May now—the Thurstons got a message, asking Sydney to go to see him as soon as she could. There was "nothing very much the matter," said the note, which he had written himself— "a slight return of the old symptoms," that was all; but it was enough to send his daughter to him without loss of time. Enough, too, to make the doctors look grave, and warn Mrs. Thurston that there was every appearance of a long and trying illness before them, unless the next day or two brought a decidedly favourable change. No such change came. Divided between anxiety for her father and for her little infant, Sydney had almost more upon her hands than she could overtake. A few days after the commencement of Mr. Laurence's illness, the Thurston household took up its quarters temporarily in Sydney's old home, that she might be the better able to give to her father the constant care and attention he required. At first he seemed to improve again, and Sydney was able to send a better report to Eugenia. But another week saw a change for the worse. Nothing *very* serious, said the doctors—nothing to cause immediate anxiety —but sufficiently discouraging, nevertheless. And then there came the usual injunction, "At all costs, the patient's spirits were to be kept up, his every wish complied with."

One morning Mr. Laurence woke out of

an uneasy sleep in a state of feverish agitation unusual to him.

"Sydney," he said, excitedly, when his daughter entered the room, "I have had a painful dream about Eugenia. It seemed to me that she was unhappy. I must see her at once. If I were well I would go to her. As it is, you must send for her. Do you think she can come to-day? I cannot rest till I have seen her."

Sydney was greatly startled, but she retained her presence of mind.

"I will see about it at once," she replied, soothingly, "and no doubt she will come immediately. I wish I had thought of it before, dear father; but we fancied you would enjoy seeing her more when you were a little stronger."

"Never mind," he said: "it will be all right if you will send at once now."

Two hours later Sydney came back to tell him it was done. A messenger had already started for Halswood. "I thought it better than telegraphing," she said; "they are so far from the station;" but Mr. Laurence did not seem to care to hear any details. He was quite satisfied with knowing that the thing was done, and before long he fell asleep again and slept calmly.

About three o'clock that afternoon a Chilworth fly drove up to the front entrance of Halswood; a gentleman alighted, rang the bell, and inquired if Captain Chancellor were at home. He was answered in the negative, the master of the house was out, would not be in till between four and five.

"Mrs. Chancellor, then?"

Disappointment again. She was not well enough to see visitors. Could the gentleman send in his message?

The gentleman hesitated. The position was an awkward one. "Is there no one I can see? No friend, perhaps, staying in the house?" he inquired at last.

A gleam of light—the footman, murmuring an unintelligible name, turns appealingly to Mr. Blinkhorn in the background, who comes forward.

"Miss Heyrecourt is staying here at present, sir—a relation of my master's," Mr.

Blinkhorn condescended to explain, going on to express his readiness to convey the stranger's card to the young lady if he would favour him with the same.

A look of relief overspread the countenance of Gerald Thurston, for he it was who had undertaken to carry the sick man's message to his daughter, Frank being hopelessly engaged in clerical duties.

"Miss Eyrecourt?" exclaimed Mr. Thurston, hunting for a calling-card; "I am very glad to hear it. She will see me, I am sure."

Mr. Blinkhorn and his satellites thought this looked suspicious, and afterwards retailed the stranger's delight at the mention of Miss Eyrecourt's name for the benefit of the servant's hall. In another minute Gerald was shaking hands with Roma, and explaining to her the reason of his sudden appearance. At first her expression was bright and cheerful; she was evidently pleased to see him again and interested in what he had to tell. But as he went on, her face grew grave—graver even than there seemed cause for.

"There is nothing immediate to be feared," Gerald said, in conclusion; "Mr. Laurence may linger for months as he is, or he *may*, it's just possible, he may recover. I saw the doctor after I had seen Sydney this morning. I thought it would be more satisfactory for Eu—for Mrs. Chancellor to hear I had done so."

"Yes," said Roma, "it was a good thought;" but she spoke a little absently, and still looked very grave. "I hope Eugenia will be able to go at once," she went on. "She is not very strong, but I think she is quite well enough to go, and I am sure she will think so. Only you know," with a smile, "she must consult her husband too, and I don't know what he will say. You see, she has been more or less an invalid for so long."

"I did not know it," said Gerald, with concern and surprise. "Indeed, I don't think Sydney does."

"Does she not?" exclaimed Roma. "Eugenia must have concealed it then. A mistake, I think. Those things always lead to misapprehension. But she is really much better now. Shall I go and tell her? She had a headache to-day, that was why she didn't want to see any one. There is not much time to spare. When did you say you must leave?"

"The best train leaves Chilworth at six; the next at 7.30," he replied.

"Well, I must tell her at once, then," said Roma. "I am leaving here myself at five. I have only been here two days, on my way, or rather out of my way, north. I spend to-night at Stebbing with some friends who happen to be going north too, to-morrow."

"You should have come by Wareborough again," suggested Gerald. "I am sure Mrs. Dalrymple would have been delighted to see you."

"Next time, perhaps," answered Roma. Then she added, with a smile, "I am quite getting to like Wareborough—or, at least, some of the people in it—though I used to think it such a dreadful place."

Suddenly something in her own words

made her blush and feel ashamed of herself. "I must go to Eugenia," she said, hastily, leaving the room rather abruptly as she spoke.

"I wonder what there is about that Mr. Thurston that always makes me behave in his presence like an underbred schoolgirl?" she thought to herself, as she went upstairs.

Barely five minutes—certainly not ten—had passed when the door of the room where Gerald was waiting opened, and Eugenia herself appeared. He had turned, expecting to see Roma again; a slight constraint was immediately perceptible in his manner when he saw who the new-comer was. The last time he had seen her had been on her marriage day. At first sight he hardly thought her much altered. She did not look ill, for the excitement of Roma's news, the eagerness to hear more, had brought a bright colour to her cheeks. When it faded again he saw how pale she really was.

"Oh, Gerald!" she exclaimed, with all her old winning impulsiveness, "how good of you to come! How very good of you!

Of course I shall go back with you at once. And Roma tells me there is no actual cause for more anxiety? You are sure of that, are you not, Gerald?"

He repeated to her word for word what the doctor had said to him that morning. She felt he was speaking the truth, and seemed satisfied.

"I expect Beauchamp in directly," she said, looking at her watch. "He will probably want to take me home himself, but I shall try to persuade him not. He is going out to dinner to-night. It will be quite unnecessary for him to come. I shall tell him he may come to fetch me if he likes."

She spoke confidently, but with a certain nervous hurry of manner new to her, and that did not escape Gerald's observation. Just then Roma joined them. A sudden thought struck Eugenia.

"You have had nothing to eat, Gerald," she exclaimed. "Roma, dear, would you ring and order some luncheon in the dining-room? I think I must run upstairs again and hasten Rachel. She is not accustomed to sudden moves."

Captain Chancellor came home from his ride about the time he was expected. He was a very punctual man. He came in at a side door, without ringing. The first sign of life that met him as he crossed the hall, was the sight, through the half-open dining-room door, of an entertainment of some kind going on within. An impromptu repast at which the only guest was a stranger, a man, that was all Beauchamp could see, for the unknown was sitting with his back to him, but as he looked, a still more astonishing sight met his eyes, Roma, no less a person than Roma, was keeping the stranger company!

Who on earth could it be? Beauchamp hated unexpected visitors, and irregular meals and "upsets" of every kind; above all he hated that anything should take place in his own house without his knowing all the ins and outs of it. Vaguely annoyed, he was turning to make inquiry, when an eager voice arrested him. It was the voice of

Rachel, a very flushed and excited Rachel. Captain Chancellor objected to the lower orders displaying their feelings in his presence, and at the best of times there was a latent antagonism between Eugenia's husband and her maid.

"Oh, sir," exclaimed the agitated damsel. "Oh, sir, you have come in. I am so glad." ("What business is it of yours?" thought her master.) "My mistress is so anxious to see you at once, sir, please."

"What is the matter? Where is your mistress?" he asked impatiently.

"Upstairs, sir, in her own room, packing," she replied, rashly.

"Packing? What in all the world do you mean? Packing, where to go to? Are you all going out of your senses?" he demanded, with increasing irritation.

But Rachel, seeing which way the wind blew, had prudently fled. There was nothing for it but to go up to Eugenia's room, and find out for himself the reason of all this disturbance.

Ten minutes later, the bell of Mrs. Chancellor's dressing-room rang sharply, and a message came down to Miss Eyrecourt, requesting her to go upstairs at once.

When Roma entered the room, there stood the husband and wife, the former looking out of the window, tapping his boots impatiently with the riding whip still in his hand; the latter by the side of a half-filled trunk, her face white and miserable, but with a gleam in her eyes which Roma had never seen there before.

"Roma," she cried, as Miss Eyrecourt came in, with a passionate, appealing despair in her voice, "Roma, he wont let me go! And my father longing so for me. Roma, speak to him."

"Roma knows better," said Beauchamp, with a hard little laugh. "Let you go? I should think not. You must be completely insane to think of such a thing. You who have been making yourself out too much of an invalid to go anywhere— why, you refused Lady Vaughan for this very evening!—to think of setting off on a three or four hours' journey with a perfect stranger—a stranger to *me* at least, whom your father sends off in this helter-skelter fashion to fetch you, because he is not very well and nervous and fanciful. I never heard such a thing in my life! I can't understand your complete indifference to appearances in the first place."

Eugenia said not a word. Roma, knowing of old the mood which Beauchamp was in, controlled her indignation, though it was not very easy to do so.

"Perhaps you will come downstairs, and hear the whole particulars from Mr. Thurston himself," she said to Captain Chancelcellor, coldly. He took the hint, and followed her out of the room. Outside, on the landing, she turned upon him. "Do not think I am going to interfere," she said quickly. "I know it would be useless. I don't take upon myself to say that she should go, that she is well enough—though, to my thinking, the distress and disappointment will be worse for her than the journey —but in the thing itself you may be right. But this I do say, that the *way* you have done it, your manner to her, is simply," she hesitated a moment, "brutal," she added, with contemptuous distinctness. "Bringing in the vulgar question of 'appearances' at such a time!"

This was her parting shot. She turned and left him, and Beauchamp, without having replied to her by word or glance, stalked away downstairs to Mr. Thurston.

He was very civil to Gerald, so civil as to make the new-comer feel that he was looked upon as a total stranger; so full of acknowledgments of the great trouble Mr. Thurston had given himself, as to suggest that the qualification "unnecessary" was in his thoughts all the time. But Gerald did not care enough for the man to be annoyed or in any way affected by his opinion; he only cared for the errand he had come upon, and his disappointment was great when he found it was to be a fruitless one. He did not attempt to hide it.

"I am exceedingly sorry that Mrs. Chancellor cannot return with me," he said; "it is very unfortunate."

"But, from what you tell me, there is no cause for pressing anxiety," said Captain Chancellor. "Mr. Laurence is not in a critical state?"

"There is no immediate danger, so at least the doctor assured me," Gerald admitted. "But my own opinion is less favourable. I do not like this sudden feverish eagerness to see his daughter: it is quite unlike Mr. Laurence. I confess, it made me very uneasy, and I dread the effects of the disappointment."

Beauchamp smiled. There was a slight superiority in his smile. At another time it might have irritated Gerald as it did Roma, who had re-entered the room.

"I can't say that I see any grounds for uneasiness in what you mention," Beauchamp said. "Every one knows how fanciful sick people are. And as for the disappointment, there need be none, I hope. I shall see my wife's medical man to-morrow, and, if he approves, I shall bring her over to Wareborough myself in a few days. A very different thing from acting without his approval."

And with this, Gerald had to be content. There was reason in what Captain Chancellor said, but his evident consciousness of being the only reasonable one of the party made it all the more irritating to have to abide by his decision.

"Mr. Thurston," said Roma, when, for a moment, they were alone, just as he was leaving, "Eugenia asked me to beg you to forgive her not coming down again, and she told me too, to thank you 'very, very much.' And will you add to your kindness by writing to her to-morrow, and saying exactly how Mr. Laurence is, and how he bore the disappointment."

"Certainly I will," said Gerald. "I will write to-night, if the post is not gone. Our post is late."

"And," added Roma, hesitatingly, "you will prevent their thinking it her fault. I mean, you will prevent their thinking her indifferent or careless, without, of course, blaming any one else, if you can help it." She grew a little confused. "It is not a case in which any one can interfere, but oh, I am so sorry for her!" she broke out.

Mr. Thurston's eyes looked the sympathy he felt, but he did not say much.

"I think you may trust me," he said at last. "I will try to explain it as she—and you—would like. And after all," he added, by way of consolation, as he shook hands, "perhaps we are rather fanciful and exaggerated. I could not help thinking so when Captain Chancellor was speaking."

It was nearly time for Roma herself to go. She went up again to Eugenia. She found her standing by the window, which overlooked the drive, watching Gerald's fly as it disappeared.

"Did he promise to write?" she asked as Roma came in.

"Yes, to-morrow, certainly—possibly to-night."

"Did you say anything more to him, Roma? Did you ask him to tell them how I *longed* to go—how it was not my fault?"

"Yes—at least, I told him how earnestly you wished to go, but that it could not be helped. It would not have done to have let them think there had been any discussion about it, would it? And perhaps Beauchamp is wisest. I blame myself for having seemed to take your going for granted, at first."

"You need not. You have been very good to me," said Eugenia. And then the two kissed each other, a rare demonstration of affection for Roma.

She offered to defer her journey to Deepthorne, to stay at Halswood as long as Eugenia liked. Beauchamp's wife thanked her, but said, "No, any 'to-do' would run the risk of annoying him," and Roma, knowing this to be true, and not a little uncertain besides what place she at present held in the good graces of the master of the house, did not persist.

So she drove away to Stebbing, and Captain Chancellor in due time departed to his dinner-party at Sir Bernard Vaughan's, and Eugenia was left alone.

Afterwards, Roma wished that she had stayed.

CHAPTER V.

THE LAST STRAW.

> Oh Lord, what is thys worldys blysse,
> That changeth as the mone!
> My somer's day in lusty May
> Is derked before the none.
> *The Not-Browne Mayd.*

THERE was no letter the next morning. "Gerald must have been too late," thought Eugenia, trying to think she did not feel anxious. But the morning after that there was none either —none, at least, that she caught sight of at first. There was one with the Wareborough postmark, but it had a black seal and was addressed to her husband, and he prevented her seeing it till he knew its contents. Then he had to tell her. It was from Frank. Eugenia never knew or remembered distinctly anything more of that day, nor of several others that succeeded it. And Captain Chancellor never cared to repeat to any one the wild words of reproach which, in the first moment of agony, had escaped her. But, satisfied though he was that he had acted for the best, there were moments during those days when Beauchamp was thankful to recall the assurance which Sydney's husband had had the generous thoughtfulness to give in this letter. "Even if Eugenia had returned with my brother it would have been too late;" an assurance which Eugenia's stunned senses had failed to convey to her brain.

This was the history of that day at Wareborough—the day, that is to say, of Gerald's unsuccessful errand.

As soon as he was satisfied that Eugenia had been sent for, Mr. Laurence became calmer. He slept at intervals during the day, and when awake seemed so much better that Sydney almost regretted the precipitancy with which she had acted on what was, perhaps, after all, only an invalid's passing fancy. But by evening she came to think differently. The nervous restlessness returned in an aggravated form. Every few minutes he asked her what o'clock it was, and she, understanding the real motive of the question, replied each time with a little addition of volunteered information.

"Seven o'clock, dear papa; they *may* be here by nine, you know;" or, "a quarter to eight; they will be about half way if they started by the later train."

Between eight and nine, to Sydney's great relief, her father fell asleep again. She dared not leave him, but sat beside him, watching his restless slumber; wearied herself, she had all but fallen asleep, too, when she was startled by his suddenly addressing her.

"Sydney," he said, "tell me—Eugenia?" His voice was clear, and stronger than it had been of late, yet he seemed to find difficulty in expressing himself. A strange fear seized Sydney.

"Not yet, dear father," she said, consolingly. "She has not come yet. But very soon she must be here."

He looked at her earnestly, as if striving to take in the sense of her words. "No," he said, at last, "no, it will be too late." Then a smile broke over his face. "Good-bye, dear Sydney, dear child. Tell Eugenia not to grieve. It is not for long."

Sydney had seen death, but never a death-bed. Death, when all the life-like surroundings are removed, when the last tender offices have been performed, and the soulless form lies before us in solemn calm; in this guise death is easier to believe in—to realise. But *dying*, the actual embrace of the grim phantom—a phantom only, thank God—she had never seen, and it came upon her with an awful shock. For some minutes—how many she never knew—she stood there beside the bed, in agonized bewilderment, almost amounting to unconsciousness. The first thing that brought her to herself was the sound of wheels rapidly driving along the street, suddenly stopping at their door.

"Eugenia!" cried Sydney, "oh, poor Eugenia! She has come, and it is too late." Then a mocking hope sprang up in her heart. "Perhaps he has only fainted," it whispered. She knew it was not so, yet somehow the idea gave her momentary strength. She rang the bell violently. In another moment her husband and the servants were beside her. But in an instant they saw how it was—the good, kind father, the gentle-spirited scholar, the earnest philanthropist had passed through the awful doorway—had entered into "the better country." And Eugenia had not come!

Sydney did not see her brother-in-law that night, but the next day he told her all—not quite all, but enough to prevent her blaming Eugenia—to fill her with unspeakable pity for her sister. To Frank, Gerald was somewhat less communicative.

"Fine lady airs and nonsense," exclaimed the curate. "Not well enough, indeed! Think how Sydney has been travelling about with her father and wearing herself out, poor child. Still I am very sorry for Eugenia. It will be an awful blow to her."

And the letter he wrote to Beauchamp,

deputing him, as was natural, to "break the sad tidings" to his wife, was kind and considerate in the extreme.

Return of post brought no answer, considerably to their surprise, for Frank's letter had contained particulars of the arrangements they proposed, among which Captain Chancellor's presence at the funeral had of course been mentioned. Sydney felt anxious and uneasy; her husband tried to reassure her by reminding her that her nerves had been shaken, and she was inclined to be fanciful in consequence.

"It must be some accidental delay," he said. "Letters seldom go wrong, but when they do, it is sure to happen awkwardly. Besides, I think it just possible Chancellor may be bringing Eugenia over. She will probably wish it."

As he spoke there came a loud ringing at the bell. Sydney started. In the sad days of death's actual presence in a house such sounds are rare. There were grounds for her apprehension. In another moment a telegram was in Frank's hands.

"From Captain Chancellor to Rev. F. Thurston.

"Is it possible for Sydney to come at once? E—— is very ill."

The husband and wife looked at each other.

"My poor Sydney," said Frank, "it is very hard upon you."

Within an hour, Sydney was on her way to Halswood. It was a strange, melancholy journey. Arrived at Chilworth, she found the Halswood carriage in waiting, on the chance of her early arrival, and drove off at once. How pretty and fresh, how mockingly bright, the country looked, in its as yet unsullied spring dress! How beautiful the park was, when the carriage turned in at the lodge, and there stretched out before her view, on each side, the broad, undulating sweep of grassy land, fringed round with noble trees! Sydney was townbred; she loved the country with the yearning, enthusiastic, half-reverent love of one who seldom breathes the fresh, pure air, to whom the country sights and sounds are fascinatingly unfamiliar. In a moment's forgetfulness she glanced at the baby by her side, asleep in the nurse's arms: "How fortunate Eugenia is," she thought, "to have her home here—to be able to look forward to bringing up her children in this lovely place." Then she remembered all, leant back in her seat, and was conscious of no other feeling save the gnawing anxiety that had accompanied her all the way.

When she reached the house, she learnt, somewhat to her surprise, that her brother-in-law was not in. He had only gone out for a stroll in the park, by the doctor's advice, having been up for two nights and being much fatigued—of course, not thinking it would be possible for Mrs. Thurston to arrive so early—was what Blinkhorn informed her, adding, in answer to her eager inquiry, as he condescendingly showed her into the morning room, that his mistress was "Better—decidedly better. Good hopes were now entertained of her recovery."

Then Sydney had an interview with Mrs. Grier, in her element of lugubrious excitement. In somewhat less sanguine terms, she confirmed the favourable report. "But the baby," she went on to say, "was in a very sad way, poor lamb!—only just alive, and no more."

"The baby!" repeated Sydney, in amazement. "I had no idea—I had no thought of a baby for a long time to come."

"Nor any one else, ma'am. It is very hard upon it, poor innocent! to have been hurried into this sad world, this valley of tears, so long before it should have been. But it cannot live, ma'am—they say it is quite impossible; and I am sure there are many of us—myself for one—that will feel it is to be envied."

"Has my sister seen it? A boy, is it?" asked Sydney.

"No, ma'am—a girl, fortunately," replied Mrs. Grier, with a curious mingling of conventional sentiment with her unworldly aspirations. "My mistress has seen it, for a moment,—this morning early, when for the first time she seemed quite conscious. It was then she asked for you, and my master sent at once. Poor dear lady! how pleased we were, to be sure."

Real tears shone in the housekeeper's eyes, and Sydney began to like her better.

"I wonder how soon I may see my sister?" she was just saying, when a step in the hall caught her ear. It was Beauchamp. The door opened and he came in —came in, looking well and fresh and handsome — offensively well, thought Sydney; heartlessly cool and comfortable.

"This *is* kind, truly kind," he exclaimed, really meaning what he said, but unable to throw off the "amiable" manner and sweet tone habitual to him when addressing any woman, especially a young one. "I had no idea you could have come so quickly. You have heard, I hope, how much better Eugenia is. All will now, I trust, go on well. She must have had a narrow escape, though," and his voice grew graver.

"Yes," said Sydney; "I am inexpressibly thankful. But," she added, "the poor little baby?"

"Ah, yes," replied Beauchamp, indifferently, "poor little thing! It's a good thing it's a girl, is it not? You would like to see Eugenia soon, would you not? The doctor said there would be no objection; she wishes it so much. I can't tell you," he added, as he led the way upstairs, "I can't tell you how thankful I have felt that I prevented her going to Wareborough that day. The shock of finding it too late on getting there would have been even worse, and after a fatiguing journey too. Yes, I am very thankful I put a stop to that."

Sydney said nothing. She did not wish to yield to prejudice or dislike, but half a dozen times in the course of this five minutes' conversation, her brother-in-law had grated on her feelings. It was very inconsiderate of him to speak so of the journey to Wareborough, which he must know had been her dear dead father's proposal. She almost wished Frank had not told him Eugenia would have been "too late." She had expected to find Beauchamp full of sympathy, and possibly of self-reproach; here he was, on the contrary, priding himself on what he had done! At least he might have had the grace to refrain from any allusion to so painful a subject. But she said nothing. And soon, very soon, she forgot all about it for the time, in the sorrowful delight of seeing Eugenia again, of listening to her murmured words of intense, unaltered affection, of gratitude and piteous grief.

"It was not the shock that did me harm," she whispered to Sydney, later in the day; "it was *remorse*. Oh, to think of what he must have thought of me! My kind, good father!"

Then Sydney, who had hitherto dreaded the subject, saw that the time had come for delivering her father's message. She did so, word for word as it had been given to her.

"And so you see, dear Eugenia," she added, in conclusion, "you need have no remorseful feeling. *He* never thought you indifferent; and had you come, it would have been too late. Frank said so in his letter."

"Thank God!" whispered Eugenia; "and thank you, Sydney. I think now a faint remembrance recurs to me of Beauchamp saying my going would have been no use. But I took it as merely a vague consolation of his own. Had I understood it properly, I might have controlled myself better, and then perhaps I would not have been ill. I don't mind for myself, but the little baby. Oh, Sydney, my poor little baby! They say she cannot live!"

She turned her great sorrowful eyes to her sister, as if praying for a more hopeful verdict; but Sydney dared not give it. She had seen the poor little piteous atom of humanity. The only wonder to her was that it lived at all.

"And it would have been such a pretty baby!" she murmured. Then another thought struck her. "Has it been baptized?" she asked.

"Not yet. We sent to the Rectory, but Mr. Dawes is away from home. Then I sent to Stebbing, and Mr. Mervyn is coming— he will soon be here. That reminds me—

let it be called 'Sydney'—my mother's name and yours."

"Will Captain Chancellor like it?" suggested Sydney, not without hesitation.

"He need not be asked," answered Eugenia, quickly. "He cares nothing about it—it is not a *boy!*" with bitter emphasis. "No, it is all my own—living it is mine—dying, doubly mine. You will do as I ask, Sydney dear?" she added, the almost fierceness of her tone melting again into gentleness.

The little creature's name never became a source of discussion. The feeble life flickered out that very night, leaving, short as had been its span, one sore, desolate heart behind it.

Yet, physically, Eugenia made satisfactory progress towards recovery. Sydney began to think of returning home, where her presence was much needed. She did not feel that after the first she was of much comfort to her sister; for as she grew stronger, a cloud of reserve seemed to envelope Eugenia —she to whom it used to be impossible to conceal the most passing fancy. To Sydney she was most loving and affectionate, never wearied of talking over old days, full of interest in the Thurstons' home-life and prospects. But of her own life and feelings she said hardly a word. It might be right and wise to say nothing, where there was nothing satisfactory to say, thought Sydney; but all the same, it made her very unhappy. Knowing of old Eugenia's inclination to extremes, she doubted if her grounds for disappointment and dissatisfaction were altogether real and unexaggerated. But she could not urge an unwilling confidence—especially on a subject of which she felt she knew too little to be a wise adviser. For her brother-in-law was almost a complete stranger to her. He was very civil and attentive to her the few times they saw each other during this week, and more than once repeated his thanks for her prompt response to his summons; but when she said she must fix the day of her return home, he did not press her to stay.

"You must come again before long," he

said, "and by that time Eugenia will be all right again. I expect my sister here in a week or two, which will cheer us up a little. It will never do for Eugenia to yield to depression. The doctors assure me she will be all right if she will keep up her spirits, and Mrs. Eyrecourt is just the person to discourage that sort of thing—low spirits and hypochondria."

Sydney sighed. She knew very little of Mrs. Eyrecourt, but she felt an instinctive doubt of her sister's "grief being med'cinable" by such doctoring.

The day before she left, a little incident occurred which broke down temporarily one side of the barrier of reserve with which Eugenia had surrounded herself. Sydney was sitting by her sister's bedside; the invalid lying so quietly, that the watcher thought she must be asleep. Suddenly an unexpected sound broke the stillness—an infant's cry, once or twice repeated, then the sort of sobbing "refrain" with which a very sleepy little baby soothes itself to peace again.

Much annoyed, Sydney rose quickly but

softly from her seat, and was hastening across the room, when Eugenia's voice recalled her.

"What was that, Sydney?" she inquired. "I was not asleep."

"I am so sorry, dear," said Sydney, looking very guilty, the colour mounting to her forehead. "I am afraid it is my little boy. You know I was obliged to bring him; but I hoped this would not have happened. Mrs. Grier gave us rooms at the other end of the house on purpose; but I suppose nurse, thinking him safely asleep, ventured along the passage."

For a minute Eugenia did not speak. Then she said, gently, "Never mind, Sydney. Perhaps it is best. Kiss me, Sydney." And when her sister's face was closely pressed to her own, she whispered, "Even to you, dear, I can hardly tell *how* terrible is my feeling of loss—loss of what I never had, you might almost say. But oh, if you knew how I looked forward to what that little life would be to me! Sydney, if you are ever inclined to blame me, pity me too. I need it sorely."

The sisters seemed almost to have changed places. Sydney could hardly answer for the tears that choked her. Eugenia was perfectly calm.

"Poor Eugenia, dear Eugenia!" said Sydney at last; "I do know a little at least of what you must be feeling. There have even been times in the last few days when I have not wanted to see my baby—when I have felt almost angry with him for looking so strong and healthy. Oh, poor Eugenia!"

Eugenia drew her sister's face down and kissed her again.

"Do you remember, Sydney," she said, suddenly, "a day, long ago, when we were putting camelias in our hair? Mine fell off the stalk, and you said you would not wear yours either, because I had none."

"Yes," said Sydney, "I remember." Then they were both silent.

"I should like to see your boy," said Eugenia, in a little—"not to-day, perhaps, but before you go. Bring him to me the last thing, that I may kiss him."

Sydney did so, "the last thing" before

leaving the next morning. And thus the sisters parted again.

Three more weeks found Eugenia, comparatively speaking, almost well again, and beginning to resume her usual habits. It was the end of May by now; surely the loveliest season of the year, when the colours are brilliant yet tender with the dewy freshness wanting to them later in the year; when there is sunshine without glare, life in abundance with no attendant shadow of already encroaching decay. A season when happy people feel doubly so from nature's apparent sympathy with their rejoicing, but a season of increased suffering to the sorrowful. Oh, but the sunshine can mock cruelly sometimes! And oh, the agony in the carols of the soulless little birds! And the flowers, even! How heartless the daffodils are, and the primroses, and worst of all, perhaps, the violets! How can you show your heads again, you terrible little blossoms, and in the self-same spots too, where last year my darling's voice cried out in rapture that she had found you, hidden in the very lane where, day by day, in childish faith, she unweariedly sought you? Does she gather spring flowers now? Are there primroses and violets in the better land? There is "no need of the sun, neither of the moon" in that country, we are told; "there is no night there," "neither death, nor sorrow, nor crying." Should not this satisfy us? But it does not. We long, ah! how we long sometimes to know a little, however little more, to see if but for an instant the faces of the children playing in the golden street, by the banks of the crystal river.

Eugenia's little baby's death had been a bitter disappointment, but in its momentary life there had been no time for the gathering of hereafter bitter associations. Yet the bright spring days added to her sadness and exaggerated her tendency to dwell upon her losses. They had been many and severe, she said to herself: the father whose affection had been tried and true; the infant in whose existence she had bound up many hopes for the future—and besides these, what more had she not lost? "Trust, hope, heart, and energy," she sadly answered.

One day, nearly a month after Sydney's visit, Beauchamp told her with evident satisfaction, that he had heard from his sister; "she hopes to be here to-morrow," he added.

"To-morrow," repeated Eugenia, aghast. She had heard something of an impending visit from Mrs. Eyrecourt, but she had heard it vaguely. Absorbed in her own thoughts, it had never occurred to her that it was likely to take place so soon, or that the actual date would be fixed without her being further consulted.

"Yes, certainly, to-morrow. Why not?" said Beauchamp, coolly. "And I am exceedingly glad she is coming. It is quite time you tried to rouse yourself a little, my dear Eugenia, and some fresh society will do you good."

"Society, Beauchamp?" answered Eugenia, reproachfully, "You cannot expect me to go into society *yet!*"

"I wasn't speaking of going out, or anything of that kind. I dare say you are hardly up to that; but Dr. Benyon says you would be ever so much better if you had some variety. When Gertrude comes, I want to arrange for going away somewhere."

"I did not mean with regard to my health," said Eugenia. "I am well enough. I meant, considering other things; how recently——" she broke off, abruptly. "I would rather have been left alone a little longer; but, of course, a visit from your sister is different from any strangers coming."

Captain Chancellor looked slightly uneasy; an intuitive feeling had warned Eugenia that something more was to come. "Gertrude is coming alone," he said; "but she asks me if we can have the Chancellor girls here a fortnight hence. They are going to stay with her at Winsley, and she would like them to be here part of the time. And of course, there is no possible objection to it? They know we are not going out just now. One or two small dinner-parties and a little croquet, or that sort of thing, will be all they will expect."

Eugenia made no reply. Beauchamp began to get vexed. "You surely are not going to make a new trouble out of such a simple thing as this?" he exclaimed.

"I don't want to make any trouble," she answered, drearily. "I must do what you tell me; but I do think it cruel of you to put this upon me. I don't expect you to sympathize in my greatest loss, but I *cannot* understand your not caring about our poor little baby."

Captain Chancellor gave vent to a muttered exclamation of impatience.

"You are infatuated, Eugenia!" he exclaimed. "Do you never look at home as the cause of half the things you complain of? It is not true that I did not care about the poor little thing. I cared as much as was natural considering the circumstances, and that it was not a boy. But I detest exaggerated sentiment. And really, you have no right to reproach me. You must know you have no one to thank for this particular trouble but yourself; your own want of self-control and wild behaviour because I had prevented your going off to Wareborough in that insane way, were the cause of it all. I did not intend ever to have alluded to it; but you provoke me, I do believe, intentionally. I cannot express the least wish of late but you set yourself against it. It never seems to occur to you that I have my share of disagreeables to put up with. Do you think the sort of life I have had the last few months was what I looked forward to, or that any man would envy me a wife everlastingly in low spirits like you?"

He left the room as he spoke, having, as usual, when he lost his temper, said more than he meant or really felt, regretting already that he had said so much, and at the same time mortified by the consciousness of his rudeness and unkindness. Eugenia remained where he had left her, some degrees more miserable than she had been before this conversation, though such painful scenes were not, unfortunately, so rare as to give any fresh direction to the current of her unhappiness. "Yes," she thought to herself, "it is all true—it has been a wretched mistake for him too. It is all true, but ah! how terrible for him to be the one to say it."

The next day brought Mrs. Eyrecourt—Mrs. Eyrecourt, in brilliant spirits and beautiful attire. For the correct number of months of mourning for her cousins having expired some time ago, she had deserted the trailing crape in which her sister-in-law had last seen her, for less lugubrious plumage. And on Eugenia's present mood, unfortunately, the bright though well assorted colours struck as discordantly as last year's sable on the feelings of the bride. But there was an unexpected pleasure in store for Beauchamp's wife. Out of the fly containing the luggage and the maids a small figure appeared. It was Floss—Floss, smaller, queerer, greener-eyed, and more defiant than ever; but internally, nevertheless, in a state of intense excitement and delight at the thought of seeing Aunty 'Genia again, hearing more dolls' stories, possibly—who could say?—seeing those venerable ladies themselves.

"Floss wouldn't come in the carriage with her uncle and me," said Gertrude, turning to Eugenia. "She is more of a little savage than ever, I fear."

"Poor Floss!" thought her aunt, as she kissed her.

Gertrude was in a very amiable mood. She congratulated Eugenia on looking so well—"Ever so much better than she had expected to see her," while wondering in her secret heart at the sad change in her sister-in-law's looks. "It must be partly her clothes," she decided, and marvelled more that her brother allowed her to wear such "atrociously made mourning." She sighed as she reflected what a different wife she would have liked to see at the head of her brother's table, and sighed again as she remembered her own short-sightedness in another direction. But her sighs were upstairs in her own room. Downstairs, she was amiability and liveliness itself. She talked, and laughed, and asked questions about the neighbours and neighbourhood, to which nearly all the answers came from Beauchamp—for in most instances Eugenia's information was at fault, her interest palpably languid. Yet when Gertrude turned from her with a patronizing "Oh, no, of course, you have not met them—it was when you were ill;" or "Ah, yes, I remember you were not there," Eugenia felt unreasonably indignant. Altogether, this first evening left her with a mortifying sensation of being an outsider in her own home; she felt again the same sensation of loneliness and isolation, of being in no wise essential to her husband's well-being, which had so depressed her the first evening at Winsley. And more bitterly than ever her thoughts went back over and over again to the irreparable past.

"Aunty," inquired Floss, a day or two after this, when she was alone with Eugenia, "are you as pwetty as you used to be?"

The stare of the blue-green eyes was rather disconcerting.

"I don't know, Floss," said Eugenia. "I daresay not, but it doesn't matter. What makes you ask?"

"What does 'falled off' mean?" continued Floss, pursuing her own train of thought.

"I wont answer silly questions, Floss," replied her aunt, her face flushing, nevertheless.

"'Tisn't silly," said Floss, indignantly. "Big people said it. Mamma said you had falled off *tewibly*, and Uncle Beachey looked cross and said it was your own fault. I don't think Uncle Beachey is nice at all. He spoke so cwoss. I thought falling off meant tumbling and hurting yourself, but it doesn't. It's something about being pwetty and ugly. And mamma said she wished she hadn't interfered once, and then somebody else who wouldn't have falled off would have been here. Does it mean about widing? Everybody says Aunty Woma looks pwetty widing, and I *know* mamma meant her."

So far, in a sort of stupor of bewildered

amazement, Eugenia had listened in silence to the child's curiously jumbled revelation. Suddenly she recollected herself.

"Floss," she said, sternly, "you must not repeat what you were not meant to hear, and I will not listen to you."

"It wasn't not meant for me not to hear. I was just playing with my new doll. I never listened behind the curtains. I never did," said Floss, "not since the day I cut the worm up, and Uncle Beachey scolded me. The day Aunty Woma said she'd go away, and Uncle Beachey was angwy. And I never told that mamma scolded Aunty Woma till she cwied. Aunty Woma didn't go away, but Uncle Beachey did, and when he comed back he bwought you, Aunty 'Genia, and I wish you wouldn't look so gwave. Please don't be angwy with me."

There was an "et tu, Brute," inflection in the child's tone which, through all her tumultuous feelings, touched Eugenia. She stooped to kiss Floss, promising her not to be angry if she would never again talk about what she heard big people say. Then she sent her away to her dolls, and sat by herself trying to think over what she had heard, calmly; trying to persuade herself the inference to be drawn from Floss's garbled communication was not what her first instinct had told her it was; trying to believe it *could* not be true that her husband had never really cared for her—that he had married her merely in a fit of mortified vanity, "out of pique."

Beauchamp was away that day. He had left home on a two days' visit in the neighbourhood, in which, greatly to her disgust, Mrs. Eyrecourt had not been invited to accompany him. Had he been at home, doubtless Eugenia, in her first impetuous excitement, would have rushed to him for confirmation or refutation of what her morbid imagination had already worked up into a plausible history of deception and concealment on his part—of cruel advantage taken of her inexperience and confiding trust—an explanation, she told herself, of his having so quickly grown weary of her, to which it now seemed to her innumerable, little-considered trifles pointed as the true one.

"Not that I blame him for loving Roma," she thought. "Oh no—not that. But he knew I was giving him my all, and he took it, sought it, knowing he had nothing to give me in return. Ah, it was cruel!"

She pressed her hands to her throbbing temples and burning eyes. It was too late in the day for any relief by tears; she felt as if she could never cry again. For a long time she sat there motionless. Then a sudden thought struck her. "I will hear the whole truth," she said, with a sudden fierce determination. "I will make his sister tell it all. There is nothing dishonourable in forcing her to tell me what he has wilfully concealed, if, as the child says, they talk together of the past, and wish now—now that I am his wife, the mother of his child" (this thought, alas! bringing no softening influence with it) "that it could be undone. Yes, I will make her tell it all, and she shall see what she has done—ruined two lives, if not three."

But through her tremendous excitement she remembered one trifling consideration. She would not betray poor baby Floss. Mrs. Eyrecourt should never know how she had learnt the truth.

CHAPTER VI.

FRIENDS IN NEED.

> Did I speak once angrily . . . .
> . . . . . You woman I loved so well,
> Who married the other ?
> R. BROWNING.

THE days were almost at their longest, but it was late enough to be nearly dark one evening, when a fly rattled along the street in Wareborough where the Thurstons lived, and drew up at the curate's door. Frank was out: he had been sent for by a dying parishioner, and had warned his wife he might be detained till late—she had better not sit up for him. Sydney had just made up her mind to act upon this injunction, and was gathering her feminine odds-and-ends about her, previous to going to bed, when the unexpected sound of an arrival startled her in the midst of her housewifely "redding up.".

She was standing in the middle of her pretty little drawing-room, her work-basket in one hand, the book she had been reading in the other, the lamplight falling softly on her fair, quiet face and deep mourning dress—a peaceful, home-like picture, it seemed to the stranger, who suddenly came in upon the scene. A tall, black figure, with veiled face and shrouding drapery, stood in the doorway. Sydney was not hysterical, so she did not scream, but for a moment or two her heart beat fast, and her breathing seemed short and irregular. Who could it be?

"Sydney," said the veiled woman, "don't be startled, dear. It is only I."

"Eugenia!" exclaimed the sister, scarcely less startled than before. "Can it be you, Eugenia? Oh, what is wrong? What is the matter?"

Before answering, the new-comer turned to the door, said a word to the servant waiting just outside—a word of directions as to paying the driver, for which purpose she handed her purse to Sydney's mystified handmaiden—then, re-entering the room, she carefully closed the door.

"Can you take me in for a night, Sydney?" she asked. "You see, I have made sure of your doing so. I had nowhere else to go to." She sat down, as she spoke, on the nearest chair: her attitude told of extreme dejection, her voice sounded faint and weary.

"Take you in, dearest? Of course we can, and with the greatest pleasure," said Sydney, warmly. "Only—only—I fear—is there something wrong?"

"Yes," replied Eugenia. "At least, I suppose you will call it something wrong. It is just that I have left him—left my husband—for ever."

"Oh, Eugenia, oh, dearest sister, do not say so. It is too dreadful to be true. It cannot be so bad as that," exclaimed Sydney, in horrified amazement. "Surely, dear, you don't mean what you say—you cannot!"

"I do, though," said Eugenia. "I left Halswood secretly this afternoon, and I never shall return there. It is done now; there is no turning back."

"And why?" asked Sydney, striving to speak calmly, half inclined to think her sister's brain was affected, yet, on the other hand, shrinking from the thought of what miserable story she might not be going to hear of terrible delinquency on Captain Chancellor's part which had driven his outraged wife to this fatally decisive step. "I don't like to ask you, Eugenia," she went on, "but I suppose I must."

"I will tell you all. I have been longing to do so," returned Eugenia. "But, if you don't mind, I should like to go upstairs and go to bed. I am *so* tired. Then I will tell you everything. May I have a cup of tea or a glass of wine? I have eaten nothing since the morning. I am so sorry to trouble you, dear," as Sydney hastened away in search of the sorely-needed refreshment. "Frank is out, I suppose?"

Half an hour later, somewhat refreshed

and revived by Sydney's care, Eugenia told her story—told Sydney "all," from the first faint misgiving as to the prospects of her married life—the first shadowy suspicion of her estimate of Beauchamp's character having been a mistaken and illusory one; down through the long, painful struggle to blind herself to the truth, through the sad history of disunion and disagreement, of ever-increasing alienation, to the discovery of to-day—the discovery that, as she expressed it, "the one thing I clung to through all—the belief in his love for me, in his having loved me at least, was but a dream too—a part of the whole illusion—of the whole terrible mistake. For he never really cared for me, Sydney. When he left Wareborough that Christmas he had no thought of ever seeing me again; he had only been amusing himself. What happened at Nunswell was a mere chance—a mere impulse. He was in a mortified, wounded state from Roma's rejection, and my evident devotion offered itself opportunely. I dare say he was *sorry* for me, too—

pleasant to think of, is it not? I see it all as plainly as possible; the only thing that puzzles me now is, how I could ever have been so infatuated as to see it differently."

"And did Mrs. Eyrecourt really tell you all this?" inquired Sydney, for Eugenia had made no secret of the sources of her information. "When you taxed her, I mean, with the inferences to be drawn from the little girl's chatter? I can hardly understand how your sister-in-law *dared* to say such things. Surely she might have tried to soften the facts!" She spoke indignantly, nevertheless she was conscious of a strong suspicion that her sister's excited imagination had had to do with the filling in of some of the details which gave colour and consistency to the whole story.

"I *made* her tell me all," answered Eugenia. "Not that she wanted to soften it, but at first she was a little frightened. Afterwards I do believe she enjoyed telling me, though all the while affecting to do it so reluctantly. She cannot understand where

I learnt what I already knew, and she shall never know. Oh, Sydney, she said hateful things! When I asked her how she could have interfered between her brother and Roma, when I told her that by so doing she had ruined *three* lives, she said something about my romantic ideas, and hinted that if Beauchamp had known that he was to succeed his cousin, when he met me again at Nunswell, he would never have thrown himself away as he did. But I don't think I minded that; it seemed too coarse to touch me. Then, at the end, she seemed to get frightened again, and tried to soothe me down. She reminded me that no wife should expect her husband's full confidence as to the past, and she said that no girl could be so foolish as to imagine that a man like Beauchamp could have lived twenty-eight years in the world without love affairs of some kind. If it had not been Roma, it would have been some one else; I should think myself fortunate I had nothing worse to complain of. I dare say there is a sort of coarse truth in it—the world is a dreadful, miserable place; and, oh, Sydney, I wish I were dead!"

There was nothing for it but to soothe and caress her into temporary calm. She was too utterly worn out to be capable of being reasoned with; it would have been cruel to attempt it. Much as Sydney felt for her—intensely as she pitied her—she could not for a moment deceive herself into thinking that Eugenia had acted well or wisely. It had been a wild impulse that had urged her to this foolish, undignified step—so her best friends would say, and the world would say yet harsher things—yet, oh, poor Eugenia, how well Sydney understood the tumult of her feelings—the peculiar agony to her nature and disposition of the wounds she had received, the bitter anguish of the disappointments she had had to endure! It was with a very sore heart Sydney left her for the night; it was with no small uneasiness she reflected on what she had to tell her husband, and tried to imagine what course he would determine on pursuing. For in certain directions Frank could see but one road; rough and thorny though it might be, he sometimes showed but scant tenderness for those who, he decided, must walk therein. He was a good man—a good and true-hearted man, but of some kinds of trial and temptation he knew as little as his own baby son.

Sydney's misgivings proved to be not unfounded. Eugenia slept till late the next morning, for the first part of the night sleep had deserted her altogether. It was so late when she woke that Frank had already left the house, Sydney told her.

"He has gone again to that sick man, and there is a meeting of some kind at one, so he will not be back till the afternoon; but he hopes to see you then," she added.

"And was that the only message he left for me? Could you explain things to him at all—do you think he enters into my feelings?" asked Eugenia, anxiously.

"He was exceedingly surprised, and of course distressed," answered Sydney, a little evasively. "We talked a great deal. Frank is very anxious about you, and very desirous of advising you for the best. Indeed he is, Eugenia; you must try to believe this, whether you agree with him or not."

"That means, he blames me, and me alone, for my misery," exclaimed Eugenia, impetuously. "You need not try to soften it to me, Sydney. Tell me all he said, plainly; though, truly, I think he might have had the manliness to say it to me himself, and not give you the pain of doing so."

"You are mistaking him, indeed you are, dear Eugenia," said Sydney, eagerly. "He is far, very far from blaming you only, and he is *very* sorry for you. All he says is, that this step that you have taken so impulsively is a sadly unwise one, and can do no good; and he says, your husband must be told where you are, immediately."

"Has he gone to tell him?" inquired Eugenia, bitterly. "He wont find him at home. Beauchamp does not return till to-morrow."

"Of course he has not gone. He would not do anything of the kind without telling you," answered Sydney, with a little wifely indignation. "What Frank has made up his mind to is this—I was just going on to tell you,—either you or he, he says, must write to your husband to-night, telling him where you are, and asking him to come here to-morrow, or whenever he can, and then things must be talked over."

"And I shall be taken home again—that is to say, if Beauchamp condescends to forgive me, like a naughty child?"

"Eugenia, don't," said Sydney, imploringly. "Frank will tell you what he thinks himself. He hopes indeed to show you that returning home is the only right course, but he does not think of you as you fancy. He is only so very anxious to show you what terrible harm may be done if this goes further, if—if it were to be talked about. For you know you have no *real* grounds of complaint."

"I have not been beaten or starved, certainly," said Eugenia. Then, with a sudden change of tone, "Sydney, I did not think *you* would have been persuaded to see things so. But suppose I refuse to be guided by Frank's advice?"

"I wont suppose it," said Sydney; "Eugenia, you will think differently after a while. You don't realise how terrible a thing you propose; you would be the last person to bear philosophically the sort of odium that always attaches itself to a woman in the position that yours would be. I do feel for you intensely; still I cannot but think there was exaggeration in this last trouble—I mean in what Mrs. Eyrecourt told you. Things may yet be happier with you. But you *must* believe that both Frank and I are earnest in our anxiety about you. Of course Frank's being a clergyman makes him express himself very decidedly, and he may seem hard to you. He has to be so very careful, too, to avoid the least appearance of—of anything that people could say ill-natured things about."

This last was an unfortunate admission.

"I quite understand Frank's feelings," observed Eugenia. "I shall act with consideration for them."

Her tone of voice was peculiar. Sydney could not understand it. "Then you *will* write?" she said, timidly, "or shall Frank?"

"He can do so if he likes," answered Eugenia. "But there is no mystery about what I have done. I left a note for Beauchamp, and one for Mrs. Eyrecourt. I made no attempt to conceal where I was going. I only came away quietly because I did not want any discussion. I should have brought Rachel with me, but she was here already. She came to Wareborough for a holiday last week. I must let her know I am here."

It all sounded as if Eugenia meant to be reasonable, but Sydney felt far from satisfied. She thought it wiser, however, to say no more at present; not to irritate her sister by attempting to extort any promises. She was rewarded by Eugenia's increased gentleness of manner. The rest of the morning passed peacefully; Eugenia seemed interested in seeing over Sydney's house, and of her own accord proposed a visit to the nursery, where it went to her sister's heart to see how she fondled and caressed her little nephew.

"And she used to hate babies so," thought Sydney. "I wish Frank could see her now. Poor Eugenia!"

After luncheon Sydney was obliged to go out for an hour. She was distressed at having to leave her sister, but the engagement was one which could not be deferred, and Eugenia assured her she "did not mind being left alone."

"I shall not be long," said Sydney; "very likely I shall meet Frank, and we shall come back together."

Eugenia kissed her as she was setting off, kissed her affectionately, and thanked her "for being so good to her." So Sydney departed in much better spirits.

She did not meet Frank; her business detained her somewhat longer than she expected, an hour and a half had passed before she found herself at her own door again.

"Is Mrs. Chancellor in the drawing-room?" she inquired of the servant, as she went in.

The girl's wits were not of the brightest at any time. Now she looked confused and frightened. "I thought you knew, ma'am," she exclaimed, "I fetched a fly immediately you had gone out, for the lady. She has gone."

"Gone!" cried Sydney, in dismay, forgetful of everything except the shock of distress and disappointment.

"She left this note for you, ma'am," added the servant.

"Perhaps she has gone home," thought Sydney, with sudden hope. She tore open the envelope.

"Thank you, dearest Sydney," said the note, "for your love and kindness. After what you have told me, however, of your husband's feelings, I cannot stay longer with you. But do not be uneasy about me. I will write to you in a day or two. I cannot tell you where I am going, for I do not know myself. I am very miserable and very desolate; but I am not so selfish as to wish to make you unhappy too.

"Your affectionate EUGENIA."

"What else is she doing than making me miserable too?" thought Sydney. "Oh, Eugenia, this is very cruel of you."

Frank came in almost immediately. He too was greatly distressed, and at first a little alarmed, and in consequence of these feelings, after the manner of men, he relieved himself by scolding his wife.

"You must have irritated her," he exclaimed. "I really thought you were more judicious, Sydney. It would have been far better to have said nothing till I came in, and then I would have put the whole before her clearly, but not so as to hurt her."

Sydney took the undeserved blame meekly, nor did she remind her husband that, in saying what she had, she had acted by his express injunctions.

"I blame myself for leaving her," she said, sadly.

Then they set to work to think what was best to do. Frank's first impulse was to trace his sister-in-law at once. There would be little difficulty in finding her, he said. It would be easy to discover the driver of the fly, and learn from him to what station he had taken her—for Wareborough boasted no less than three—and, once certain of the railway by which she had travelled, the rest would be easy.

"For it is not," he said, "as if she had any particular reason for mystery. She is sure in any case to write to us in a day or two."

In this Sydney agreed, so after talking it over a little more, they decided it would be best to take no such steps as Frank had at first proposed.

"The publicity of making any inquiries about her," he said, "is one of the things most to be avoided. Besides I hardly feel that I have a right to take any such steps. I will write to Chancellor at once; I shall write very carefully, you may be sure. But don't be uneasy, Sydney. We shall hear from her in a day or two, you'll see."

Sydney sighed. There was nothing for it but patience.

"I wish Gerald were at home," she thought. But he was not, and the next day or two passed very anxiously with Eugenia's sister.

The elder Mr. Thurston was at this time away on a fishing expedition, having allowed himself the rare luxury of a fortnight's holiday. He had been fishing up, or down, the stream from which Nunswell takes its name, and for the last few days had made this little watering-place his headquarters. It was a Friday when Eugenia left Wareborough, and late on the following day, Gerald, having returned to Nunswell, there to spend Sunday in decorous fashion, was strolling in the public gardens—the very gardens where he had sat and talked with Eugenia, some fifteen or sixteen months ago —the same gardens where, the very next day, "time and chance combining," Beauchamp Chancellor and she had met again— when something familiar, something indefinably suggestive in the gait and bearing of a lady walking slowly a little way in front of him, caught Mr. Thurston's attention. He was thinking of Eugenia at the moment. The resemblance of the figure before him to the object of his thoughts struck him suddenly as the explanation of his vague sensation.

"If Eugenia were dead," he said to himself, "I should shrink from dispelling the illusion, as no doubt many a ghost could be dispelled; but believing her to be alive and well, I think I should like to see the face of that tall, black-robed lady. Very likely she is old and ugly." And half smiling at his own fancies, he quietly quickened his steps so as to overtake her. It was not difficult to do so. The part of the garden where the two were walking was retired and unfrequented. There was hardly another person within sight. As Gerald's increased pace brought him quickly on a line with the solitary lady, the sounds of his footsteps caught her ear. Just as he passed her, she mechanically turned her face in his direction. Mr. Thurston's nerves were under good control, but the start of almost incredulous surprise at seeing his own wild fancy realised, betrayed him into a sudden exclamation.

"Eugenia!" he said, impetuously, "Eugenia, is it really you?" And even while he spoke, he looked at her again more closely, with a new fear of being the victim of some extraordinarily strong accidental resemblance. But it was not so. Eugenia's surprise, though considerable, was less overpowering than Gerald's, and she answered him composedly enough.

"Yes," she said, with a little smile—a smile that somehow, however, failed to lighten up her face as of old—a poor, pitiful, unsatisfactory attempt at a smile only. "Yes, it is certainly I. Are you very much astonished to see me? Where have you sprung from?"

"I have been fishing down the Nun," he replied. "Are you staying here? Is Captain Chancellor here?"

"Yes and no," she answered, with a very forced attempt at playfulness. "I am staying here, but alone."

"Alone!" he exclaimed in surprise.

"Yes, alone," she repeated. "Why do you cross-question me so, Gerald? Why do you look at me so? I am not a baby. You are as bad as Frank. I wish I hadn't met you. I didn't want you to speak to me. I don't want any one to speak to me. I have no friends, and I don't want any."

Then suddenly, to his utter amazement, she finished up this petulant, incoherent speech by bursting into tears. They were the first she had shed since she left Halswood; and once released from the unnatural restraint in which they had been pent up, they took revenge on it by the violence with which they poured forth. The position was by no means a pleasant one for Mr. Thurston, though he did not share Captain Chancellor's exaggerated horror of tears, or believe with him that they were invariably the precursors of hysterics. "Something must be wrong, very wrong, I fear," he thought, and his unselfish anxiety and genuine pity for the suffering woman by his side quickened his instincts on her behalf. For a minute or two he walked on beside her in silence. Then, as they were approaching the more frequented part of the gardens, and her sobs gave no sign of subsiding, he spoke to her — quietly and kindly, but with a slight inference of authority in his tone, which, excited as she was, she instinctively obeyed.

"Suppose we turn and walk back again a little way," he said. "You have over-tired yourself, I am afraid."

She did not speak at once, but turned as he directed. He could see now that she was making strong efforts to control herself. When she thought that she could trust her voice, she spoke.

"I am ashamed of myself, Gerald, utterly ashamed of myself," she said at last. "What must you think of me? I suppose I have over-tired myself. I have been walking about here nearly all day. I had nothing else to do."

"And you are really alone here?" he inquired.

"Yes, except my maid, Rachel Brand; you remember her?—I am quite alone."

"And how—how is it so?" he was going to ask, but stopped. "No," he went on,

"I will not presume on our old friendship to ask questions you may not care to answer; only tell me, Eugenia, can I be of any service to you?"

"None, thank you," she answered sadly. "No one can help me. Even Sydney no longer feels with me—that is why I am here alone."

"Your doubting Sydney makes me doubt if things are so bad as they seem to you," he said, with a little smile.

"Don't doubt it," she said quickly. "They could not be worse, Gerald," she added, after a little pause. "You have known a good deal about me—more perhaps almost than any one else. I will tell you the worst sting of my misery—I have come to know that my husband does not care for me—that he never has done so—that never a woman made a more fatal mistake than I when I married."

Mr. Thurston started violently; a sort of spasm of pain contracted his forehead— pain of the past, not of the present, so far as he himself was concerned.

"Eugenia," he said, gravely, "from you, these are terrible words."

"I know they are," she said bitterly, "but I believe they are true. I married under a double delusion. But I believe I could have endured the one great disappointment of finding how I had over-estimated my—my—never mind. I say, I think I could have learnt to bear my many disappointments, and make the best of my materials, had my other belief, my sheet anchor, not failed me as it has done. By the light of what I now know, I can see that for some time its hold has been growing feeble and uncertain on me, and in consequence my strength has decreased, my good resolutions have faded, till now I have nothing to hold to. I hardly care where I drift—what does it matter?"

"What does it matter?" broke out Gerald, indignantly. "Eugenia, do you know what you are saying? Oh, you foolish, presumptuous child! Does duty depend on inclination, do obligations cease to bind us when they become difficult or painful? Allowing that you have been deceived, allowing that you have found your life essentially other than you expected, does that set you free from responsibility? The world is bad enough already, but what it would be if we all regulated our conduct by your principles, I should shudder to think. And the cowardliness of it too! Eugenia, I thought you a woman incapable of thus deserting your post!"

The colour had mounted to Eugenia's pale face, but the tears had ceased to flow. "You are very hard, Gerald," she said at last. "You cannot possibly estimate my position correctly. I left my husband because I felt I should grow worse if I stayed, grow worse myself, and make him grow so too. For my belief in him once shattered, *no* link remained between us, no common ground on which we could meet. What could be the end of such a life?"

"What will be the end of the one you have chosen for yourself, and forced upon him?" asked Gerald. "Duties once discarded, we are not immediately allowed to console ourselves with others of our own choosing, as you will find to your cost. What are you intending to do—why did you come here?"

"I don't know. It just came into my mind. I meant to wait here till something could be settled for the future. My husband is not the sort of man to force me to return: he is too proud. I don't want any money from him. I have enough of my own. I suppose some sort of separation could be agreed upon. I have heard of such things."

She spoke with a sort of dreary indifference.

"And, in the meantime, why come here alone? Why not go to Sydney."

"I did," she said. Then she went on to tell him why she had left his brother's house. "Frank evidently disapproved of me altogether," she remarked, "and even Sydney seemed to think I greatly exaggerated things."

"As to that I can't judge. I don't wish to judge," said Gerald, quickly. "Of course,

I should suppose you have reason to trust implicitly the sources of the information on which you acted?" he looked at her keenly as he spoke. Eugenia slightly changed colour.

"My own instincts are not likely to deceive me," she said, hotly. But her honesty pushed itself in, with some misgiving. "There is one person I should like to see—a person I trust thoroughly. Of course she can only confirm what I discovered, but still, strictly speaking, I suppose I should have her confirmation before I can say I am *quite* sure of what I acted upon."

"Do you mean Miss Eyrecourt?" said Gerald.

"Yes," answered Eugenia, looking up with some surprise at his correct guess.

"I am glad you trust her," he said, briefly. They had turned again by now, and from time to time other strollers passed them, glancing at them in one or two cases, with the slight, indolent curiosity with which watering-place loungers inspect each other. Eugenia's veil was drawn down, but her tall figure in its deep mourning garments could not but be somewhat conspicuous. Gerald chose the quietest paths, but still he grew uneasy. He did not like to leave his companion till he had seen her safely to her own door; his terror lest she should suspect him of suggesting the expediency of their separating, made it impossible for him to find any plausible excuse for saying good-bye: yet at every step he realised more painfully the awkwardness that might attend their recognition. "Ever so many Wareborough people come here," he reflected, "and who knows but what by this time there is full hue and cry after the missing Mrs. Chancellor. It is frightful to think what she is exposing herself to," and, glancing at her as the thought crossed his mind, some irritation mingled with his pity. "She is too absorbed to understand it, but something *must* be done at once."

"Does Sydney know where you are now?" he asked.

"No," she replied, "not yet. But I am going to write to her to-night."

When they had reached the house where she had taken rooms, Mr. Thurston held out his hand in farewell.

"Wont you come in, Gerald?" Eugenia asked.

"No, thank you. I have letters to write, and the post leaves early. You must take care your letter is in time."

"Yes," she answered, absently, adding, "If you wont come in to-night, will you come and see me to-morrow? I—I will try to think of what you have said, if it is not too late."

"Then you don't think me hard and cruel?" he said, gently.

"No, oh no. I only thought you *could* not understand."

"This much I understand," he replied. "You have suffered a great deal, where many women would have suffered little. It is your nature to do so. Therefore, I dread for you, with unspeakable intensity, the deeper suffering you would bring upon yourself—most of all the knowledge, which, sooner or later must come to you that you had done wrong, grievously wrong—for it is not a case where duty is difficult of recognition."

She did not answer, but sometimes silence is better than words. She went upstairs to the neat, bare, unhomelike lodging-house drawing-room, and sat down to think. She thought and thought so long and so deeply, that poor Rachel knocked several times before she was heard, and, unfortunately, it was past post-time! So no letter reached Wareborough the next morning.

CHAPTER VII.

ROMA TO THE RESCUE.

That he has his faults cannot be doubtful; for we believe it was ascertained long ago, that there is no man free from them.—CARLYLE.

IT is dreary work—perhaps no one who has not had personal experience of it can imagine how dreary—to find oneself really alone in a strange place, with no customary daily duties to compel one's attention, however unwilling; no chance of a friendly face looking in to break the monotony of the empty day; no anticipation even of the post bringing distraction in the shape of news, good or bad. Such had been Eugenia's life for two days at Nunswell, and already in these two days she had many times been on the point of saying to herself she could not stand it much longer.

"And is this to be my life?" she thought with a shiver, for, in the excitement of flying from her home, she had taken no account of the loneliness and dreariness that lay beyond. Now, the unconcealed disapproval of her nearest friends, the realisation of her anomalous position alone in lodgings in a strange place, were already bringing home, even to her uncalculating inexperience, something of the personal suffering, the bitter deprivations, the indefinite suspicion which must attach themselves to even the purest and noblest of women, once she voluntarily abandons her home. There may be cases, doubtless there are such, where a wife has no choice, where duty itself, deaf to all suggestions of expediency, relentlessly points out the way to abandonment of the post bravely battled for to the last—but such cases are rare, and the women to whose bitter experience they fall must have suffered too terribly to be sensitive to loneliness, or monotony, or half-averted looks. Not so was it with Eugenia Chancellor. What she had learnt from her sister of Frank's opinion of her conduct had wounded her to the quick; her only idea had been at once to relieve her friends of her unwelcome presence, but she had altogether failed to realise the desolation and hopeless depression which seized upon her before she had been many hours in the Nunswell lodgings.

The morning after she had met Gerald, she woke with a slight sensation of expectation. She hoped she should see him again; she wanted to talk to him, and tell him how she had thought over his words; she did not feel indignant at his plain-speaking, for it was not contemptuous and unsympathizing like Frank's, but sprang, she could not but feel, from genuine anxiety for her good, from single-minded incapability of advising her to act otherwise than as he believed to be right. "Still it is often impossible," she thought, "for one person to judge of right and wrong for another," and, more out of a feminine determination to prove herself justified in what she had done than from any vehement desire to persevere in her present course, she prepared herself mentally with a whole string of unanswerable arguments, of well-sounding sophistries with which to compel her old friend to acknowledge how exceptional was her position, how principle and self-respect, and unselfishness even, had driven her to this apparently undutiful step.

It was still early when Rachel tapped at her mistress's door. "A letter, ma'am," she announced, as she came in.

"A letter!" exclaimed Eugenia, not without excitement, "it must be a mistake. No one knows where—I mean, I have not sent my exact address yet." But notwithstanding her words, her heart beat with vague, unreasonable hope—what could it be?—could Sydney have found her out, and be coming to her at once?—could Beauchamp himself be on the way to beseech her to return to him, to entreat her forgiveness for all he had made her suffer, to assure her that this last misery, this worst trouble of all, had somehow or other been a mistake, a mischievous exaggeration of his sister's? As one possibility after another suggested itself to her imagination, Eugenia's heart beat faster and faster. "Give it me quickly, Rachel," she said impatiently. But as the girl brought it to her, she remarked, "It is not a letter by the post, ma'am. It is only a note—from the Spa Hotel, I believe," and Eugenia's hopes died within her. It was only a note—a few hurried words from Mr. Thurston—beginning "My dear Mrs. Chancellor," to inform her of his being suddenly obliged to leave Nunswell on business, and to express his regret that he should not see her again. It was dated the previous evening. "As if he could have got any business letters after he saw me last night, and as if he would be likely to travel home about business on a Sunday," thought Eugenia, with a bitter incredulity; "no, he has just thought it over, and agrees with Frank. They don't want to have anything more to say to me."

And this day was even more miserable than its predecessors. She would not go to church, she dreaded now even the thought of a stroll in the gardens; she sat alone in the dull drawing-room all day with no books to read, no letters to write, nothing to do, nothing to hope for. And when bedtime came and she knelt, more from the force of old habit than from any expectation of comfort, guidance, or peace of mind, to pray to the Father who understands us all so much better than we understand ourselves, she started back from the appealing attitude in horror. For the only prayer which rose with any spontaneity to her lips was that she might sleep and never wake again.

Hours passed and still she lay awake, feverish, restless, and yet exhausted. When at last she fell asleep it seemed to her afterwards that it must have been close to morning. And the longed-for unconsciousness brought her but little repose, for it was broken by anxious distressing dreams, of which the only one she could recall with any distinctness was the last before she awoke. She dreamt that it was again the night of her father's death, she herself was hastening to him with Gerald Thurston; they were driving furiously along a road of which some features seemed familiar to her, though at the same time she felt perfectly certain she had never traversed it before; and from time to time her companion added to her feeling of indescribable bewilderment by asking her if it would not be better to turn now and go the other way. She never seemed to answer him, but every time he made the suggestion, the invisible driver appeared to respond by turning sharply, and driving away faster than ever in an apparently opposite direction. Suddenly the scene changed, and Eugenia found herself by her father's bedside, in the room she knew so well; and she became conscious of the strange dual existence familiar to us all in dreams, for while there in her father's presence, waiting for her own arrival, she was yet driving on with Gerald; again she heard his curious monotonous inquiry, "Don't you think we had better turn now and go the other way?" Another change; she was now in the old state bedroom at Halswood, where she had spent the night of her arrival there; she was still watching by a bedside, still waiting for her own appearance. Then the sound of the carriage wheels, of which all this time she had been conscious, grew louder and louder; she heard them rattling up the smooth carriage drive at Halswood as if it were a paved Wareborough street. A clock began to toll, the figure in the bed by which she was watching seemed to move, and a sudden horror seized her. In her dream-agony she rushed to the door of the room, and found it locked; in despair, it seemed to her, she screamed aloud with frantic vehemence, "Let me out, let me out;" and a voice, which she recognised as her husband's, answered from the other side—"Too late, too late. Better turn now and go the other way." And at this crisis she awoke.

It was broad daylight. Rachel was standing by her bedside, a cup of tea in her hand.

"What is the matter?" asked Eugenia,

confusedly. Then, coming a little to herself, she sat up and looked at the girl. "My head is aching dreadfully," she said, laying it back among the pillows as she spoke; "is that why you have brought me some tea, Rachel? Oh, no; of course you could not know. But there is something the matter, Rachel; you look as if there were."

"No, indeed, ma'am, there isn't; nothing, that is to say, except your head being bad. I was awake very early this morning, and I had my breakfast sooner than usual, and I thought you might like a cup of tea."

"I am very glad of it," said Eugenia, languidly. "But what made you get up so early. Had you a bad night too?"

"Oh, no, ma'am, thank you. I was wakened by some visitors arriving unexpectedly about five o'clock. One visitor, at least. A young lady."

"What an odd time to arrive," observed Eugenia, carelessly. But, glancing at Rachel as she spoke, something in the girl's manner again caught her attention. "*Who* is the young lady?" she asked, quickly. "Is it some one to see me—is it my sister?"

"No, ma'am, it is not Mrs. Thurston," replied Rachel, evidently afraid lest her words should cause disappointment. "It could not be Mrs. Thurston, for she will only get your address this morning, you remember, ma'am. But it *is* some one for you. It is——"

"It is I," interrupted a voice at the door. "May I come in, Eugenia?" and in a moment Roma Eyrecourt stood by the bedside. "You poor child," she went on, hurriedly, as if to cover some embarrassment, and without giving Eugenia time to speak; "how burning your hands are, and your head too! I am not going to teaze you, dear. I have come to do exactly what you tell me, except go away. You wont send me away, Eugenia, will you?"

There was some anxiety in her tone; she leant over towards Eugenia as she spoke, and looked earnestly into her face with her beautiful, bright dark eyes—not keen or contemptuous now, but tender and loving, and almost entreating in their expression. The struggle, if there were one, was quickly over with Eugenia. She threw her arms round her friend's neck and kissed her warmly. "It is very, very good of you to have come," she whispered. "I know it is pure goodness that has brought you. I have tried to fancy I hated you, but I don't. I love you and trust you. But, oh, Roma, I have been so miserable!"

"Too miserable, a great deal too miserable. I can fancy it all," said Roma, sympathisingly. "But, Eugenia, you do look so tired. I am sure you have not slept well. Do try to go to sleep again, and try to believe you are not going to be so miserable as you think. I will talk to you as much as ever you like when I see you looking better. I will tell you everything—what made me come here, and *anything* more you like to ask me, if you will do what I tell you now. I have one or two letters to write for the early post. I will come back in a little, I promise you."

Soothed in spite of herself by Roma's kindness, comforted by the feeling that she was no longer alone, that one person, at least, in the world, still loved and cared for her, Eugenia fell asleep, and slept peacefully for two or three hours. Miss Eyrecourt, meantime, wrote her letters: one was addressed to Captain Chancellor at Halswood, another to Gerald Thurston, at Wareborough, a third to old Lady Dervock, whom she had quitted at rather short notice. Once or twice in writing she seemed somewhat at a loss.

"I don't want to exaggerate things," she said to herself, "but I really should not be surprised if Eugenia had a bad illness—brain fever, or something of the kind. However, I can judge better when I see her again."

Roma's fears were not fulfilled. Eugenia was much better when she saw her again. By the middle of the day she was up and dressed, and eager for the promised conversation. The mystery of the new-comer's sudden appearance was easily explained.

The "business" which had necessitated Gerald's leaving on Saturday night had taken him all the way up to Deepthorne, whence he had returned accompanied by Roma herself. It had seemed to him the best thing to do; he felt certain that he might rely on Miss Eyrecourt's friendship, and he felt certain too that in the end Eugenia would not blame him for his interference. By dint of hard travelling they had managed to reach Nunswell early on Monday morning, thence by the very next train, Gerald, already due at his post, had returned to Wareborough. This was all, so far, that Roma had to tell. Of what had taken place at Halswood she was in utter ignorance. "I have not heard from Gertrude for more than a week," she told Eugenia. "I half thought of writing to her just now while you were asleep, but I decided not to do so till I had spoken to you. I have written to your husband though, Eugenia," she added, with a little hesitation.

"To Beauchamp," exclaimed Beauchamp's wife, her cheeks flushing; "oh, Roma, why did you? Could you not have waited for that till you had spoken to me?"

"No, Eugenia," said Roma, gently but decidedly, "I purposely wanted to write *before* seeing more of you. It was not betraying your secret, for Mr. Thurston told me you had let your sister know where you were, and of course Beauchamp would go to her to inquire about you. I merely wrote to tell him that I was with you, ready to stay as long as you want me."

"I don't mind Beauchamp's knowing where I am," said Eugenia. "It will make no difference. He is not likely to seek me, for even if he cared about me, he will be too angry to take any such step."

Roma thought differently. Beauchamp's regard for appearances was likely to be a powerful motive with him, but she was wise enough to keep this consideration to herself, and to direct her attention to the root of the matter.

"How do you mean, 'if he cared about you?'" she asked, quietly. "Do you doubt his caring for you?"

"Roma!" exclaimed Eugenia, reproachfully, the tears rushing to her eyes, "how can you ask me? You, of all people!"

"You must tell me exactly what you mean, Eugenia," said Roma, anxiously. "Half confidences are no use in such a case, and I, in return, promise to tell you what I believe to be the exact truth."

So Eugenia told her all; more fully even than to Sydney she related the whole history of her hopes and disappointments, her golden anticipations, and the bitter realities in which they had ended. And Roma listened with a gravely attentive face, striving to the best of her power to distinguish between fact and fancy, between Eugenia's actual grounds for unhappiness, and her morbid inclination to exaggerate them. It was not for Roma so impossible as it might have been for many to arrive at a just comprehension of the state of matters, for the character of the one of the two persons chiefly concerned had been long ago gauged by her, that of the other had interested her greatly, and now every word and look and tone assisted her to a fuller understanding of its lights and shades, its beauties and defects. When Eugenia at last left off speaking, Miss Eyrecourt sat silent for a minute or two. Eugenia's heart was beating fast with anxiety. "Roma," she said at last, imploringly, "speak to me, do."

"I was only thinking how best to put in words what I want to say," said Roma. "Listen, Eugenia. I would say it was very wicked of Gertrude to tell you what she did, if I supposed that she at all realised what she was doing, or how you would take it. However, don't let us speak of her. I would rather not. She has been very kind to me, and she is more silly and small than malevolent. As to what she told you, it was a mixture of truth and falsehood, but the part that you cared about so deeply was untrue. It is quite untrue that Gertrude's interference separated Beauchamp and me. It was not required. I refused to marry him because I did not care for him in that way in the least, and also because I did not believe, and never shall, that he cared for me either. Even if I had cared for him, I don't know but what my dread of vexing Gertrude, of seeming to repay her kindness by ingratitude, would have been strong enough to stop me; but that was *not* the reason. I simply did not care for him, except in a sisterly sort of way. And he— he fancied he cared for me, but he never did. It was greatly out of contradiction, and also because my indifference piqued him —he was so spoilt wherever he went, so sought after and petted! But I think I know the worst of him, and you may believe me, Eugenia, that he never cared as earnestly, as *truly*, for any woman as for you. I regretted your marriage, because, matter-of-fact as I am myself, I saw how different you were—I feared there would be sorrow in store for you—I feared Beauchamp would not understand you—but all the same, I never liked him so much as when I found how he *did* care for you. He is not a grand character, Eugenia; I dare say what you tell me you suspect may have been true—that he thought it was very grand of him to marry for love, notwithstanding his great prospects, and I have no doubt Gertrude helped him to think so. But, all the same, he did marry for love, and he loves you still; and, dear Eugenia, you will come to see, I do believe, that there is still a fair share of happiness waiting for you. No one will ever have the same power for good over Beauchamp as you, and even if you begin again with little hope or heart, encouragement will come; all the more quickly, perhaps, because of your faint expectations. Now I have told you exactly what I think. I have gone against the old advice never to meddle between husband and wife. I allow that you have had a great deal to bear, not a little to complain of. But, knowing Beauchamp as I do, I must say he has had something to bear too. In the first place, he is innocent of your having imagined him a different character from what he really is; he could not possibly understand it if it was told him. There has been a sort of playing at crosspurposes; for you have not made the best of him from your mistaken notion of the material you had to work upon. *Now*, you can face things. Leave the past, and decide bravely to do the best with the present."

The tears were running down Eugenia's pale cheeks: "You forget, Roma," she said, sadly. "I have no present. I have cut myself away from it. I believe all you say, every word of it. I mean, I believe *you*. But if, as you allow, Beauchamp has not understood me hitherto, how could he ever understand the feelings which made me leave him? He must be a different man from what I now believe him to be if what I have done does not estrange us more than ever. For no mere surface peace would satisfy me, Roma. I mean, I could not agree to go back and begin again, merely for the sake of appearances, knowing that in reality there was no possibility of happiness for us."

"We shall see," said Roma. "Sometimes things turn out quite the other way from what we expect. But I do think, Eugenia, you should make up your mind to do whatever you come to see is right for you to do, and never mind about Beauchamp's motives for being willing, if he prove so, to meet you half way."

Eugenia did not answer, and Roma thought it as well to leave her now to think things over in her own way. In her heart Miss Eyrecourt was not without a hope that this crisis might prove a turning-point; that the shock of finding Eugenia gone might open her husband's eyes to some part of the unhappiness she had endured, and that the way in which Gertrude had acted might lead him to a clearer understanding of the danger of her influence in his household. "Gertrude is sure to clear herself if she possibly can," thought Roma; "still Beauchamp must see she at least did not try to do any good. Besides, he must be conscious of how he has allowed her to speak of Eugenia, and how he has spoken himself. I wonder what happened when he came home and found his wife gone."

This was what had happened. It was on Thursday that Mrs. Chancellor had left

Halswood, where her husband was expected to return the next day. But the next day came and went, and it was not till pretty late on Saturday afternoon that he made his appearance. Mrs. Eyrecourt in the meantime was suffering from no more painful feeling than annoyance, and some amount of indignation at her sister-in-law's unceremonious behaviour. Anxiety she felt none, for Eugenia had by no means allowed the whole depth of her feelings to appear during her conversation with her husband's sister, and the note which was given to Gertrude on her return home from a drive that Thursday afternoon, in explanation of her hostess's absence, had been carefully worded by Eugenia, and only left on her sister-in-law's mind the impression that she herself must be held of small account by her brother's wife if some unexplained summons from her Wareborough friends was considered of sufficient importance to justify so unheard-of a breach of hospitality.

Beauchamp's non-appearance the next day irritated her still further. She was by no means in the sweetest of tempers when Captain Chancellor came home. He came back in a more than usually kindly frame of mind towards his wife. He had enjoyed his visit very much. Everybody had been very civil to him, and several people had inquired pointedly for Eugenia, whose troubles and serious illness had awakened the sympathy and interest—sincere and genuine so far as they go—which, after all, selfish and conventional as we nineteenth-century people are supposed to have become, are not yet difficult to awaken in the hearts of many of those among whom we live. Lady Hereward had been of the party, and her peculiar interest in the young mother's bereavement had caused her to single out Beauchamp in a gratifying manner.

"I cannot tell you," she had said to him, drawing him aside for a moment—"I cannot tell you how much I have been thinking lately of that beautiful young wife of yours, Captain Chancellor. I was very nearly writing to her when I heard of her—her disappointment, but I feared it might seem intrusive. Will you tell her so? And whenever she feels equal to it, I do hope you will bring her to spend a few quiet days with me. You must be very good to her—you will forgive an old woman's impertinence?—you must be *very* good to her. No doubt you are, but I doubt if even the best of husbands can *quite* enter into her sorrow. It is not to be expected they should, perhaps. And following so quickly on her father's death too! Ah, yes, it was very sad! And she has no mother! Give her my messages, and tell her of my sympathy, and be very patient with her, even if her grief seems exaggerated. There, now, I have kept up my character as a meddlesome old woman, have I not?"

But Beauchamp felt by no means offended. The interest was too evidently genuine, the sympathy too womanly for the words to annoy. And then the speaker was Lady Hereward! Captain Chancellor thought over what she had said, and was all the better for it.

No one was to be seen in Eugenia's

sitting-room when he reached home on Saturday afternoon. "She must be out," he thought; and the sound of Mrs. Eyrecourt's voice as he passed an open window confirmed his supposition. He was hastening out to join them by the door opening from his own "den" on to the sort of terrace below, when a letter, addressed to him in Eugenia's handwriting, placed conspicuously on the mantelpiece, caught his eye. In another moment he had opened and read it. His bright complexion turned to a gray pallor; a look of wild distress replaced the expression of smiling indifference habitual to him; all the nerve and spring seemed to melt out of his bearing; for "she has gone out of her mind," was the first thought that occurred to him—"grief has driven her insane," as Lady Hereward's words returned to his mind. "Good heavens! and this note is dated Thursday! What may not have happened by now?" Then his sister's voice, gay and careless as usual, again reached his ear. "Gertrude must know it. What is she thinking of? What is the meaning of it all?"

A sort of giddiness came over him. He had to sit down for a moment to prevent himself falling. Then he went forward to the window from which steps led to the walk below, and called to Mrs. Eyrecourt.

"Gertrude," he said, "come here at once. I want you."

Full of her own grievances, which the sight of her brother recalled freshly to her mind, Mrs. Eyrecourt hardly relished the authoritative summons. She came up the steps slowly, calling to her dog, whose company she much preferred to that of her daughter.

"So you have come back at last, Beauchamp!" she said, as she drew near him. "I was very nearly setting off home this morning, I can tell you. I wonder what you asked me to come to see you for!"

Her pettishness was quite lost on her brother.

"Gertrude," he said, excitedly, as if he had not heard her words, "do you not know, or *do* you know about Eugenia? What has happened?"

"What has happened?" she repeated, looking a little startled; "nothing that I know of, except that she has gone to her friends at Wareborough—her sister, or aunt, or somebody—for a day or two. I suppose she often goes there, does she not? though I certainly thought she might have waited till my visit was over."

"Is *that* all you know?" said Beauchamp, impatiently. "Do you not know with what intention she left this—that she went, never to return?"

"Good gracious!" exclaimed Mrs. Eyrecourt, now for the first time taking alarm. "You don't mean to say she has run away—run away *with* some one? How frightful! What a scandal! Oh, Beauchamp, how terribly you have been deceived!"

"Take care what you say, Gertrude," said Captain Chancellor, sternly. "Run away *with* any one—my wife—Eugenia! What are you thinking of? Read that!"

He thrust into her hand the letter he had found on his mantelpiece, and while watching her read it, he almost laughed, notwithstanding his distress, at the utter incompatibility of his sister's coarsely commonplace supposition with the perfect guilelessness, the transparency and innocence, he had often been half inclined to look upon as but a part of his wife's childishness and inexperience.

Eugenia's note to her husband was as follows:—

"I am going away because I am too hopeless and miserable to bear my life longer. Hitherto I have clung to hope and to you through all my suffering, believing that at least you *had* loved me. Now I know the whole bitter truth. I am going to my own friends. I will agree to any arrangements you like to make, but I do not want any money, except what I have of my own. I cannot think that you will in any way miss me, but I trust you will be happier without me than you have been with me.

"EUGENIA."

Mrs. Eyrecourt did not speak when she

had finished reading this. Beauchamp, observing her closely, fancied she looked pale and frightened.

"Can you explain any of this to me?" he asked, impatiently. "Has anything happened in my absence, to explain it? Or must I think she has gone out of her mind?"

Gertrude hesitated a little. "There was —we had a rather disagreeable conversation the day you left," she began. "I don't know who in the world could have put it in her head—*truly* I don't, Beauchamp—but all of a sudden Eugenia challenged me with having been the cause of your *not* marrying Roma, and by some peculiar reasoning of her own, from that she went on to argue that I was the cause of your hasty proposal to her, which she seems to look upon as the misfortune of her life."

"And what did you tell her?"

"What could I tell her but the truth? She seemed to have a very fair notion of it to begin with. I could not have deceived her. Certainly she is the most hot-headed exaggerated person I ever knew. She talked of having been deceived and all sorts of things. She must have been infatuated to think that you, with your prospects— and altogether—could have *deliberately* chosen her, or that your friends could have approved of your doing so, though of course both you and they were too honourable to try to draw back once the thing was actually done."

Captain Chancellor laughed. There was a slight incredulousness in his laugh which made Gertrude very irate. "Then what you have told me is about the general substance of what you told her?" he said.

"I suppose so," said Mrs. Eyrecourt, sulkily. "I did not begin it. I do not consider myself in any way responsible for what she has done. She seemed all right again at luncheon, and as you must have seen, I never even associated this foolish fit of jealousy of hers with her sudden visit to her friends."

But Beauchamp was not yet satisfied. For almost the first time in his life, he felt that he had his sister in his power, and he used it to the utmost. Little by little he extracted from her a full account of what had passed between her and his wife, including what she had told Eugenia of her really mistaken impression of the true relations that had existed between himself and Roma Eyrecourt, and when he had learnt all that she had to tell, he turned from her with a bitter "Thank you, Gertrude. You have certainly done your best to ruin any chances of happiness I had. I never before had a conception how spiteful a spiteful woman could be. You disliked Eugenia from the first, because she was my choice and not yours, and in the pleasure of making her miserable you have cared little what became of me."

Mrs. Eyrecourt was so offended that she first burst into tears, and then decided upon setting off to join Addie and her mother that very afternoon, leaving Floss behind her till she sent directions for her journey home. Captain Chancellor did not care. Before his sister had fixed her train, he was half-way to

Wareborough, where, however, disappointment awaited him in the shape of the Thurstons' complete ignorance of Eugenia's whereabouts. The interview with his wife's relations threatened at first to be a stormy one, for, in his increasing anxiety and perplexity, he was more than half inclined to blame them for this new complication. But they were patient and judicious; the sight of his unfeigned distress inclined Sydney to judge him more leniently than she had ever done, and new hopes began to spring in her heart, that if only Eugenia were with them again, all might yet be well. In the end, Beauchamp went home again to Halswood, by Frank's advice, to wait there quietly till they heard from their sister.

"I am certain we shall have a letter from her to-morrow or Monday," said Frank, "for even if she were ill, her maid Rachel, who, we were glad to find, is with her, would write. And it is better for you to go home, and look as if nothing were wrong. Your staying here would only make a talk, and I shall telegraph instantly we hear."

So Beauchamp went home—home to the desolate house where Eugenia had felt so sure he would never miss her; and the loneliness and anxiety and wretchedness of the next two days brought him face to face with some truths hitherto but little recognised or considered in his pleasure-loving, self-regarding life.

And after all it was Roma's letter, reaching him on Tuesday morning only, which first brought relief to the fears growing almost more than he could endure, for, by some mischance, Eugenia's unlucky note to her sister, too late for Saturday's post from Nunswell, was not received at its destination till this same Tuesday morning.

At first sight of Miss Eyrecourt's letter, Captain Chancellor could hardly believe his eyes. "*Roma* with her," he exclaimed; "Roma, of all people! How can I reconcile that with Gertrude's story?"

Incomprehensible as it was, however, the news was marvellously welcome. Half-an-hour later came Frank Thurston's promised telegram, and that very afternoon, hardly to her surprise, Rachel brought word privately to Miss Eyrecourt, that Captain Chancellor wished to know how he could see her.

"He does not want my mistress to be told of his arrival till he has seen you, ma'am," said Rachel; adding discreetly, "of course with her not being very strong it might startle her, not expecting my master so soon."

CHAPTER VIII.

O SI SIC OMNIA!

"Und dennoch wohl ûns, wenn die Asche treû
Der Fûnken hegt, wenn das getäuschte Herz
Nicht müde wird, von Neûem zû erglüh 'n!"
UHLAND.

"EUGENIA," said Roma, when they were sitting together later in the day, "I have something to tell you."

"What?" asked Eugenia.

"Some one is coming to see you—this evening or to-morrow morning, if you would like that better."

"Who is it, Roma?" asked Eugenia, the colour rushing to her pale cheeks. "Not—not Beauchamp?"

"Yes, it is Beauchamp," answered Roma. She had risen from her seat and now stood beside Eugenia, looking down at her with an expression of mingled anxiety and sympathy.

"Oh, Roma, you must have asked him to come, your letter must have brought him," exclaimed Beauchamp's wife in great distress. "I know you meant it well, dear Roma, but you should not have done it. I don't want to see him just yet. I have been trying to make up my mind to do what I suppose must be right—to offer to go back to him, and do my duty as his wife. But you don't know how difficult it will be. Oh, so difficult! He will never in the least understand the feelings that made me so miserable; he will think it was all bad temper, or low common jealousy of his having ever cared for *you*; oh, I see it all so plainly! Of course I will ask him to forgive me—ah, how gladly I would do so if I thought he could understand what he really has to forgive—it is not that I shrink from. But I see that during the rest of our life together I shall stand at such a hopeless disadvantage: he will not be able to believe in my real wish and determination to do my best; it is my own fault, I have brought it on myself, but that does not make it less bitter. This that I have done—this leaving him and my home, will be constantly rising up in judgment against me in his mind—it will never seem to him that anything was wanting on *his* side. I do mean to try, Roma, I do indeed, but all the spring has gone out of everything. Oh, how lonely it will be!"

Roma let her finish speaking without interrupting her. Then she said gently—"I think you see things at their very worst, Eugenia. I think there are feelings and motives in Beauchamp which will make your life easier than you now imagine. But I don't think my saying so will do much good. About his coming, however, I must explain that it was entirely his own doing. My letter did not bring him. I did not say a word in it but what I told you. And even if I had not written, Beauchamp would have been here by now, for your brother-in-law had sent him your address."

"*He* need not have interfered," said Eugenia, haughtily.

Roma smiled. "He meant it for the best, I have no doubt," she said. "You are sore and uneasy just now, Eugenia, and no wonder, but after awhile you will see things more brightly, I feel sure. But now, what about your seeing Beauchamp? He will be calling this evening to ask; he said he would. Would you rather wait till to-morrow morning?"

"I don't know," said Eugenia, irresolutely. Then, as a new thought struck her, "Have you seen him then, Roma?" she asked.

"Yes," answered Miss Eyrecourt. "I have seen him, and had a very long talk with him—the longest talk, I think, I ever had with any gentleman! But I don't think his wife will be jealous," she added, with a bright smile, which, in spite of herself, extracted a faint, shadowy reflection of itself from Eugenia.

Just then there came a ring at the bell.

"There he is," said Roma; "well, Eugenia?"

"I will see him now," said Eugenia, suddenly. "It is better—my putting it off might only irritate him more."

Roma kissed her without speaking, and left the room.

In the few minutes that passed before Captain Chancellor came upstairs how many painful anticipations had time to rush through Eugenia's brain! She was determined to go through with what she had promised to Roma and to herself to attempt: she would humble herself to the utmost that she could truthfully do so; she would ask her husband's forgiveness; she would own that she had taken up, with exaggeration and bitterness, Mrs Eyrecourt's version of the past. All this she would say: she owed it to her own self-respect to do so, hopeless as she felt of any good effect it might have on her future, little as she anticipated that it would awaken any generous or tender feelings towards her in her husband's heart. She pictured to herself the cold air of superiority with which he would receive her confession; she recalled the unsympathising contempt with which on several occasions her impulsive endeavours to draw nearer to him, to understand him better, had been thrown back on herself with a recoil of indignant mortification—and she said to herself that her fate was a very hard one.

There came a sort of tap at the door, and in answer to her tremulous "come in," Captain Chancellor appeared. She was standing by the table, in the same attitude as that in which Roma left her. She looked up as Beauchamp closed the door, and came forward. To her surprise, she perceived at once that he was looking ill and careworn, and that his bearing was by no means free from agitation. She was so surprised that she forgot what she had meant to say first of all; she opened her lips mechanically, but no sound was heard: then a sort of giddiness came over her for a moment, and half unconsciously she closed her eyes. He was beside her in an instant. "Eugenia," he exclaimed, "Eugenia, how ill you are looking! My poor darling, I may not have understood you—I have been a blind, selfish, careless husband, but oh, my dear, you should not have fancied I was so bad as not to care for your suffering! I did care—I do care. Your leaving me has half broken my heart. Will you not come back and try me again? Will you not believe in my love for you? Truly, it has always been there, though you doubted it."

Where were all Eugenia's carefully considered words of confession? "Thus far have I done wrong, but no farther; to this extent have I been wanting in my wifely duty, but not beyond." She threw her arms round her husband's neck, and careless of possible repulse she burst into tears. "Beauchamp," she said, simply, "I am very sorry for what I have done wrong. I will try to please you better in the future if you will forgive the past."

"We will *both* try again," he said, kindly. "Not that you did *not* please me, my dear child. Your only fault was—was—well, perhaps, as I have sometimes told you, you expected a little too much; your ideas were a little bit too romantic for every-day life. The best of husbands and wives knock against each other's fancies now and then, you know, and it can't be always like a honeymoon,"—Eugenia winced at this a little, a very little,—"but, all the same, I don't see why our chances of being happy together are not quite as good as other people's. You will gain experience, and I, I hope, will learn to understand you better. And I think that's about all we can say. I am very thankful to have you again safe and well, and the next time you make yourself miserable about anything, come and ask *me;* don't go to other people, who see nothing except through their own prejudices. Gertrude didn't mean to make mischief; all the same she did so, as I told her. But Roma has put all that right?"

"Yes," said Eugenia, "I—*we*—can never thank her enough for what she has done."

"She says," pursued Beauchamp, with unwonted humility, "I should have told you all about that old affair with her. I was very nearly doing so once, I remember, but—I don't know how it was—I was bothered at that time, and I liked to keep you distinct from it all. I was bitter about Roma for a good while, and I disliked the subject. But, Eugenia, no suffering I have ever had to bear in my life has equalled that of the last few days."

They were silent for a minute or two. "I must say," Captain Chancellor went on, speaking more in his usual tone, "the Thurstons behaved very sensibly in not making any fuss. Nothing would have been so odious as any absurd story getting about." But, happening to observe the pained expression of Eugenia's face, he changed the subject, and went on to talk of some plans he had in his head of going abroad for a time, taking Eugenia to visit many places so far known to her but by name. "It would be the best way of making you strong again," he said. "We might even spend next winter out of England, if we liked."

And, notwithstanding the unexpected encouragement she had met with in her new resolutions, it was a relief to Eugenia to be freed from the anticipation of an immediate recommencement of the life at Halswood, hitherto so lonely and uncongenial. She was touched, too, by the evident consideration for her happiness which prompted this new scheme, and Beauchamp, on his side, felt rewarded by her gratification for the amount of self-denial which the proposed plan entailed on him.

So when Roma rejoined them she quickly saw that her hopes had not been groundless; already the expression of Eugenia's face had grown brighter and less despondent than she had seen it for long.

"Was I not a true prophet?" she said, to Eugenia, when they were by themselves again. "Are not things more hopeful than you expected?"

"Yes," said Eugenia, thoughtfully, "they are; and it is you I have to thank for their being so, Roma."

"No, don't say that," interrupted Roma, quickly. "I don't like you to say so, because I want you to do Beauchamp justice. There is more to work upon in him than you were inclined to think, and you, as I told you before, have more power over him to draw out his best than any one else ever had or could have."

"But still it is your doing," persisted Eugenia, affectionately; "for who else but you could ever have opened my eyes to see this, or at least to look for it?"

A new feeling had wakened in her heart to her husband. From the ashes of the old unreasoning, wilfully blind, headstrong devotion had arisen a calmer, more tempered, more enduring sentiment. As yet she was hardly conscious of its existence; its component parts she could certainly not have defined. She only said to herself, "I don't know how it is, but, somehow, what has passed to-day has made me feel *sorry* for Beauchamp. I don't think hitherto any one has taken much pains to draw out what Roma calls 'his best.' And I am so weak and foolish and full of faults, how can I hope to do it? Yet, somehow, I think I *do* hope it."

They all left Nunswell the next day,

Roma travelling with them as far as Wareborough only, where she had promised a short visit to her cousins, the Dalrymples; Beauchamp and his wife returning to Halswood, there at once to commence preparations for their visit to foreign parts.

Eugenia trembled a little as they drew near the spot which, but so few days before, she had quitted with something very like despair in her heart. There was a mingling of almost superstitious apprehensiveness in her shrinking from "beginning again"—with new motives, new hopes, new patience—in the very place which had witnessed the woful failure of her first essays, the cloudy ending to the too brilliant promise of the dawn of her married life. But these half morbid feelings she was wise enough to keep to herself.

"I only hope," she thought, "that Mrs. Grier will not think herself bound to receive me in state after so short an absence. If she does I shall take it as a bad omen. She is a very good creature, but I shall never forget her first reception."

So it was with some little apprehension that Mrs. Chancellor looked out of the carriage as the front of the house came in sight. She knew Mrs. Eyrecourt had gone; it had never occurred to her that poor little Floss had been temporarily left behind. Her surprise was great, her relief and pleasure extreme, when, almost before the carriage had stopped, she heard her own name shouted in the little girl's peculiar pronunciation: "Aunty 'Genia, Aunty 'Genia, you have comed back! Kiss me quick! You never said good-bye when you wented away, and I cwied so! Please don't never go away any more!"

The tears were not very far away from Eugenia's own eyes, as she lifted the excited little mortal in her arms, and kissed the eager, flushed face.

"Dear little Floss," she said, "I am so glad to come back to you;" and even Beauchamp was struck by the little scene.

"What an eccentric little creature it is," he said to his wife, when, Floss's rhapsodies having subsided, she said good-night and went off to bed " as good as gold." " Who would have thought that Gertrude's child could have hugged away as vehemently at anyone as Floss did just now."

And the child's demonstrative affection put it into his head to make an unexpected proposal to Eugenia. "How would you like to take Floss with us?" he said. "I have no doubt Gertrude would be enchanted to let her come, and the child's maid is French, which would be an advantage. You see we shall not be moving about at any uncomfortable speed; you are not strong enough for it, and that sort of thing is not my idea of travelling for pleasure. When there is no need for hurry, much better take it leisurely."

Eugenia was delighted; she knew, though she never told it to anyone, the indirect influence for good which Floss's innocent championship had had upon her life, and the idea of the child's happiness was pleasant to her. Mrs. Eyrecourt was delighted; so delighted that she wrote back accepting her brother's offer, as if no shadow of anything disagreeable had ever disturbed the harmony of their intercourse. It suited her particularly well to have Floss disposed of for the present, as she was anticipating a round of visits in which a child would have been rather an encumbrance, while yet, for the sake of appearances, she could not make up her mind to leave the little girl alone at Winsley for many weeks at a time. It looked well, too, to be able to tell her friends that her brother and his wife, "having no children of their own," had taken such a fancy to her little daughter that they had begged leave to take her abroad with them for the winter; for Gertrude had sense enough to know that "family jars" are, of all things, the most undignified and "vulgar," and she had endured some perturbation of spirit of late as to the probable nature of her future terms with her Halswood relatives.

"I am so glad you are going abroad," she wrote; "it will be the very thing to set up Eugenia's health and spirits. By-the-bye, I must not forget to send all sorts of kind messages from Addie and Victoria and their mother. The girls were sorry not to see you at Halswood as was arranged, but of course they quite understand my explanation about Eugenia's not being well enough to receive them, and they hope to pay their visit some other time" &c. &c.

Some people—for of course in the neighbourhood of Halswood as elsewhere there were to be found human beings with superfluous energy to spare from the management of their own concerns, which they apparently conceived it to be their duty to bestow on those of others—some people thought it very odd and absurd of Captain and Mrs. Chancellor to burden themselves with a child on their foreign tour. It was so odd as only to be explicable by the comprehensive assertion of Mrs. Chancellor's being, to say the least, "very odd altogether." For notwithstanding all the care that had been taken to guard against outside remark, some amount of gossip had oozed out concerning Eugenia's hasty flight from Halswood. Servants, the very best of them perhaps, will but be servants. It was not in Mrs. Grier's nature to refrain from lugubrious head-shakings and mysterious allusions when she found that her young mistress had actually left home without any explanation to herself, the vicegerent of the establishment, of the reasons for this sudden step; it was not in the unexceptionable Blinkhorn's nature to refrain, at the first table at least, from comment upon his master's state of anxiety and dejection during the days of uncertainty and foreboding which succeeded his return home. And the natures of the various inferior functionaries in the Halswood household, being neither better nor worse than are ordinarily met with in their respective capacities, the rolling stone of gossip, contrary to the adage, grew and gathered as it went, till but few of the great houses in the neighbourhood, none certainly of the tea-tables in the little town of Chilworth or of the less pretentious Sunday afternoon entertainments in the farmhouses on the estate, but had their own pet version of the Halswood scandal.

Of this, however, the principals in the little drama were, as is not unfrequently the case, in happy ignorance. As to the Chilworth edition of the story, as to the village chatter, they were of little consequence. They lived their appointed nine days, then died a natural death. But as to the more discreetly veiled, but nevertheless the far more insidious, whisper that went the round of "the county," there is little saying where it would have stopped, how deep might not have been the social injury it would have caused to impulsive, reckless, innocent Eugenia, had it not suddenly received its death-blow from an unexpected but irresistible hand. It came to Lady Hereward's ears, how or whence matters little, that the wife of the master of Halswood, "the girl with the beautiful face" which somehow had recalled the memory of the long years ago dead and buried little Alice, the young mother whose little baby had died, had somehow or other done something which threatened to get her "talked about." And the good old woman rose to the occasion. "I think you are not aware, my dear Lady Vaughan," she said, the first time the subject was publicly alluded to before her, "in fact, I am quite sure you *cannot* be aware that the young lady of whom you are speaking is a valued friend of mine, for I am certain you would not intentionally hurt my feelings or those of any one. Mrs. Chancellor has passed through much sorrow, and she has my deepest sympathy. The report to which you allude is an exaggerated version of the simple fact that she was called away rather suddenly in her husband's absence to some of her own friends. When she comes home again strong and well, as I hope she will, it will give me great pleasure to introduce her and any of my friends who have not yet met, to each other, for I hope she will be often at Marshlands." Then she changed the subject; but this was the last that was heard, publicly at least, of "Mrs. Chancellor's elopement," for Lady Hereward had queened it to some purpose during her forty years reign in the county.

It was in the latter part of July that Beauchamp and his wife left home. They stayed a little time in town, then proceeded by easy stages to Switzerland, intending there to spend the remainder of the summer and the early autumn, and when the colder weather drew near, to turn their steps to some one of the winter nests in the south of France. Their programme was carried out even more fully than they had intended. Winter came and went, though they learnt it only by the shortening and then lengthening again of the soft, sunny days; spring and summer, chasing travellers and swallows away once more to less sultry regions, followed; autumn returned, and Christmas, in the unfamiliar garb he wears by the shores of the blue Mediterranean, had passed by yet again, with his all-the-world-over greeting of "glad tidings and great joy," before there was any talk of Halswood being again inhabited by its owners. Before that time came, Floss had learnt to chatter French like a magpie, Eugenia had come to doubt if she after all sufficiently appreciated the inestimable privilege of being "English bred and born," and Beauchamp, on his part, was beginning to wonder if he would be equal to keeping his seat across country next season, after his long sojourning in the tents of Kedar, otherwise regions where "le sport" was alluded to with the uncomprehending bewilderment with which we used to discuss the fascination of the feast of Juggernaut —where a day with the Pau foxhounds furnished the only procurable pretence of a run.

At last the time for their return home was fixed. It had been in July they left England; it was not till the April "next but one" that they found themselves again within her shores, their party augmented by the presence of a French bonne, with a flapping white cap and a very satisfactory "worldly-looking" baby, a great boy of four months old, a most respectable son and heir to the hitherto ill-fated Chancellor estates. At first Eugenia's disappointment that the little creature was not a daughter was great; but this feeling she expressed to no one, well aware that sympathy therein was hardly to be expected. She had learnt a good deal, she was learning every day more and more of the wisdom, the necessity of making the best of the materials with which she had to work; slowly, painfully was coming home to her the interpretation of the dream, the lesson of the great "life's trial" in which so rashly, so ignorantly she had engaged. "Love" for her had not been "clear gain," viewed by the light of the dim knowledge of to-day; but in the wiser afterwards "the sun will pierce;" the follies, the failures, the mistakes, the delusions will be lost in the beautiful whole, may indeed prove to have been essential to its perfection.

Not that Beauchamp Chancellor's wife said or thought all this to herself; she speculated and theorized and philosophized much less than of old; she lived more in the present, taking life, as we all must take it sooner or later, if it is to be endurable at all, in a day-by-day fashion, leaving the "huge mounds of years," the bewildering mazes of whys and wherefores, past and future, to be considered "by-and-by"—by-and-by, when surely we shall see things somewhat more clearly, more justly, more divinely, but a by-and-by which will never come to us if, dissatisfied with the fair promise of its far-off beauty, we seek to grasp its shadowy substance before the time.

So, in a sense—must it not always be but in a sense?—Eugenia was happy. Happier perhaps possibly, because she thought less about being happy than in the old days. She had seen before her in imagination a dreary road; to her surprise, ever and again as she walked along, fresh flowers began to spring by the wayside—little unobtrusive blossoms, hardly distinguishable till her foot had all but crushed out their tender life; tiny buds of brightness and sweetness, bringing many an unexpected spot of colour or breath of fragrance into her daily life.

She grew to be very thankful that her

child was a boy; she learnt to be grateful for every link of sympathy between her husband and herself, she tried her utmost to strengthen and rivet each one of these; and though, apparently, at least, her efforts often failed, sometimes, on the other hand, she was rewarded by success surpassing her most sanguine hopes.

"He is not a grand character," Roma had said, justly, "but, all the same, there is a great deal of good in him; and of all people, you, Eugenia, have most power to draw out and strengthen this." And these simple words Beauchamp's wife henceforth never allowed herself to forget.

They reached Halswood safe and well on a lovely spring evening. There stood Mrs. Grier, her black silk dress relieved for once by some cheerful pink ribbons, tears of joy in her eyes at the non-fulfilment of her many gloomy prophecies. It was indeed, as she took care to inform her mistress, "a day she had little expected ever to see." But Eugenia could smile at her now, as she assured her that "the luck had certainly turned" with the arrival of the great crowing baby who was to bring life and brightness to the old house.

And before long Halswood looked more cheerful than it had done for many a day. Mrs. Eyrecourt's anxiety to resume the guardianship of her little daughter was not so overwhelming as to be allowed to interfere with her plans for the season. She had just taken a house in town for her usual three months, so she contented herself with "a mere glimpse" of the travellers as they passed through, expressed herself delighted with the improvement in the child's manners and appearance, and yielded without much pressing to the proposal that Floss should accompany her friends home and remain with them till the summer. "The country is much better for children certainly," said Mrs. Eyrecourt. "I shall feel happier for Floss not to be so long in town. I only wish I could go down to Halswood with you myself, but it is impossible. I must be in town as much as I can now, so that dear Quin can spend his Saturdays and Sundays with me."

But though Gertrude could not spare time to welcome the absentees back to Halswood, Roma could. She joined them there within a week of their arrival, and for a few pleasant days Sydney and her belongings joined them too. Poor Sydney's holidays were not many, but her busy life seemed to suit her; her fair face was as calm, her voice as sweet and even, as in her girlish days; and when she and Frank went away, back again to smoky Wareborough, they were cheered by the thought that their intercourse with Eugenia promised to be frequent and cordial. Not much private talk had passed between the sisters; Eugenia was charier of confidences than had once been natural to her, but Sydney was satisfied.

"She is much happier than I ever hoped to see her," said the younger sister to her husband. "It is not exactly the *sort* of happiness I should long ago have imagined would have contented Eugenia; somehow, even though I feel so thankful and relieved about her, I could hardly prevent the tears coming to my eyes when I looked at her. She must have suffered so much, Frank (though outwardly things have been so prosperous with her) to be so changed."

"She has had to learn her lessons like other people," said Frank, oracularly.

"But isn't it wonderful how she adapts herself to her husband?" said Sydney. "He is improved, I must allow; but there *cannot* be much sympathy between them, and Eugenia must know it."

"No doubt she does, but better women than Eugenia," replied Frank, with a spice of his old antagonism, "have had to get on with less. And Chancellor's by no means a bad fellow after all; many a man would have had less patience with Eugenia's freaks and fancies than he. I always told you they'd shake into their places some day. By-the-bye, you must remind me to give that invitation to Gerald. I hope he will go, for more reasons than one."

Sydney smiled. "I hope so too," she said.

CHAPTER IX.

INSUPERABLE OBSTACLES.

But, Edith dead!—*Too Late.*

GERALD THURSTON did go to Halswood. Whether he did so knowing that there he would again meet Roma Eyrecourt is a secret that has never been divulged; whether in suggesting to her husband that he should invite Sydney's brother-in-law Eugenia was influenced by malice prepense has never transpired. Be these possibilities as they may the event they would have foreshadowed came to pass; and in this fashion.

Once, during the absence of the Chancellors on the Continent, Mr. Thurston and Miss Eyrecourt had met again. It was during one of Roma's flying visits to the Dalrymples. They had seen each other several times, had talked a good deal on a subject interesting to them both—Eugenia—and from that on one or two occasions had drifted into other talk, had found out insensibly a good deal about each other's thoughts and tastes and opinions, had discovered various remarkable points of coincidence in these directions, various no less impressive points of disagreement which both felt conscious it would have been pleasant and satisfactory to discuss further. All this talking no doubt might even then have led to a definite result, but for the prepossession with which each mind was guarded. Roma, unbeliever though she professed herself in the constancy of any man's devotion, yet made one exception to her rule. She believed, or told herself, with perhaps suspicious frequency and decision, that she believed in the unalterable nature of Gerald's feelings towards Eugenia.

"It is the only case, out of a book that is to say," she would repeat to herself, "I have ever even heard of, where a man kept faithful to his first ideal. Not that she even turned out to be his ideal, from what he has told me; but she was and still is herself. I believe he would be content to serve her unthanked all his life, and she will never have the faintest notion of it! Ah, yes, things are queerly arranged. But I am very thankful I was born matter-of-fact and easy-going, not likely to break my heart for even the best of men."

Gerald's prepossession was of quite another nature. He did not think it impossible that, had he dared to show his growing regard for this heartless young lady, he might not have succeeded in winning that which she was so fond of declaring she was not possessed of. But his head was perfectly full of the notion that, though personally she might in time have learnt to care for him, his position would prove an insuperable objection. "As if *she* would ever consent to live at Wareborough," he said to himself. "Ah, no, it is utterly out of the question." And so, with the burnt child's dread of the fire, he refrained from indulging in tantalizing speculations on the possibility of overcoming these taken-for-granted prejudices on Miss Eyrecourt's part, and from time to time congratulated himself on the skill with which he had preserved intact his peace of mind and on the strength of self-control which permitted him to enjoy a good and beautiful woman's friendship where a nearer and dearer tie was impossible.

But there came a day when his self-satisfaction received its death-blow, when he was fain to confess that after all he was neither wiser nor stronger than his fellows. He had been more than a week at Halswood. He had come there little intending or expecting to remain so long, but the days had passed very pleasantly; his hosts were so cordial, Miss Eyrecourt so friendly and companionable, that, having no pressing business on hand, he had been persuaded to linger on from day to day. It was not very often that he found himself alone with Roma, but one afternoon, some other visitors having left, it happened that they two were thrown on each other for entertainment.

"Shall you mind, Roma, if we leave you and Mr. Thurston alone to-day?" Eugenia had asked her friend after luncheon. "Beauchamp is so anxious to drive me out with the new ponies—he has driven them several times, and says they go so beautifully! And the pony carriage only holds two and little Tim, the groom, behind, and I think perhaps Beauchamp would be disappointed if I did not go."

"Of course you must go," said Roma, brightly. "I don't mind in the least. I will take Mr. Thurston a tremendously long walk, and see if he isn't much more tired than I when we come home. Men are so conceited about that sort of thing."

Eugenia laughed. She was leaving the room, but a sudden impulse seemed to come over her. She turned back to the table where Roma was sitting writing, and kissed her gently.

"What is that for?" asked Roma. "Am I particularly good to-day?"

"No, yes. I mean you are always good," answered Eugenia. "I am very happy to-day, and I always feel as if I should thank you when I feel so." Roma looked up with a grateful look in her dark eyes. ("It is nice of you to say so, but I don't deserve it," she interrupted. "Yes you do," said Eugenia, and then went on with what she had been speaking about.) "It was something Beauchamp said this morning that made me happy. I needn't tell you it all, but just a little. He asked me, Roma, if I didn't think we were getting to be very happy together, and he said, 'At least, Eugenia, you make *me* very happy, and I think I am getting to understand you and your ways of thinking about things better. I am learning to see how selfish I was—a while ago, you know. But I trust all that is over.' Then he said something else, I don't know what put it into his head—something about baby and how we should bring him up, and the future. Roma," she broke off, suddenly, "if Beauchamp were to die now I should miss him terribly. I am so *glad* to feel so, for there was a time when I *couldn't*, when my life stretched before me like a long slavery. Don't think me wicked to speak so—you understand me?"

"Understand you, dear Eugenia? Yes, thoroughly," said Roma. "And years and years hence I trust and believe you will feel as you say you do now, yet more strongly. I don't think the sort of happiness you feel is likely to fade or lessen," she sighed, half unconsciously as she spoke.

Eugenia looked at her affectionately. She seemed on the point of saying something more, but changed her mind and, kissing Roma again, left the room.

How it came about they could neither of them in all probability have exactly related. They went the long walk Miss Eyrecourt had determined upon; they talked of every general subject under the skies, avoiding at first, as if by tacit mutual consent, any of closer personal interest. But after a while, somehow, Mr. Thurston came to talking of himself, of his life, his hopes, his disappointments and failures. He was not by any means an egotistical man. Roma could not but feel flattered by his confidence; she listened with undisguised interest. Suddenly, to her surprise, he alluded to the first time they had met.

"It is curious to look back now to that evening, is it not?" he said. "You were the first lady I had spoken to for, I may say, years. Out there I was completely cut off from any intercourse of the kind. And what a fool (I beg your pardon, Miss Eyrecourt) you must have thought me! Do you remember how I bored you with my confidences? I assure you I never remember our conversation without feeling inclined to blush, only you were so very kind—*that* part of it," he added, in a somewhat lower tone, "I don't want to forget."

"You need not want to forget any of it," said Roma, blushing, however, herself as she spoke; "I certainly did not think of you as you imagine. It has always been very pleasant to me to think that—that you thought me, even at first sight, trustworthy—fit to talk to as you did. The only unpleasing part of the remembrance to me is the thought of how it all ended for you, how terribly quickly your dreams faded. Forgive me," she went on, hastily, "I am afraid I have said too much. I have never alluded to it before."

"I like your alluding to it," said Gerald. "I like the feeling that you understand it all. It doesn't hurt me in the least now. It is wonderful how one grows out of things, isn't it?—at least, hardly that; how things grow into one till one is no longer conscious of their existence.

I am a part of all that I have met.

You remember? Of course Eugenia had a great influence upon me. But for her I should probably have been quite a different sort of man. But still I can see the good it did me now without any bitterness. I am inexpressibly thankful that she is so much happier, that she seems to be growing into—*her* life, as it were. When she was unhappy I must confess I was bitter—bitter to think I had no right to interfere. But that has all past by. I am rather lonely, that is about all I have any right to complain of. If she had not married it might have been different—there is a sort of doggedness about me—I believe I should have gone on hoping against hope. But as it is, I feel it rather hard sometimes."

"What?" asked Roma, in some bewilderment.

"Why, that I should be doomed to stay outside always, as it were. You don't suppose I have any dislike to the idea of being happy like other people? You don't suppose it is from choice I remain homeless and lonely, do you, Miss Eyrecourt?"

He looked at her half laughingly, yet earnestly too.

Roma's face fell. Then after all, she thought, her one hero was no hero; already his love for Eugenia was replaced by some other apparently equally hopeless attachment. It was disappointing.

"Why do you look so grave?" he inquired. "Have I offended you?"

"Offended *me!* What have I to do with it?" she replied. "Of course not. To tell you the truth I felt just a little disappointed—a nice confession for an unromantic person to make—that—that you *had* 'got over it,' as it is called, so completely. You were my model of constancy. I shall think life more prosaic than ever now. And, to turn to prose, what a pity you a second time made an unlucky venture! Could you not have been more prudent? That is to say, if the obstacles whose existence you infer *are* insuperable. As to that, of course I can't judge."

She quickened her steps a little as she spoke. It seemed to Gerald she was eager to make an end of the conversation. Amused, yet much annoyed at her misapprehension, his wish to right himself in her eyes drove him further than he had intended.

"Miss Eyrecourt," he began, not without a slight irritation in his tone, "I wish you would do me justice. Is it possible you don't understand me? Do not you see that one of the things which *most* attracted me, which drew forth my admiration and gratitude, arose from the very strength of my care for Eugenia? It was that which first drew us together—your goodness to her, I mean—it was that which showed me how generous and noble you are. And yet, unfortunately, your knowledge of my feelings to her is one of the very things that make me hopeless, even if there were no insuperable practical objections. Not that I would have concealed the old state of things from you in any case had you not happened to know them, if I had ventured to try my chance with you. But they were forced upon you so unfortunately. It would be impossible for you ever to think of me in a different light. How could I ever convince you that the heart I offered was worth having? It must seem to you a poor wretched battered-about thing—not that, of course, it was ever worth *your* having."

Roma stopped short. Hitherto she had kept up her rapid pace. She stopped short and turned round so as to face

Mr. Thurston. He saw that she was very pale.

"Are you in earnest?" she said, very gravely. "Do you mean what you are saying? I do not altogether understand you to-day, Mr. Thurston. It would have been more in accordance with my notion of you if, allowing that you *are* in earnest, you had simply and manfully put the question to the test, instead of first imagining 'insuperable obstacles' and then putting them into my mouth. You place me very awkwardly. At this moment I solemnly assure you I do not know if you would like me to say, 'Mr. Thurston, I will marry you if you will ask me,' or not."

Notwithstanding, her seriousness, with the few last words she had difficulty in repressing a laugh. Gerald's face flushed deeply, angrily almost, as she spoke, and a quick light came into his eyes—a light, however, not altogether of indignation.

"I *would* have asked you months, years ago," he said, "had I not believed that my doing so would have been looked upon as presumption—would have put an end to the friendship I have learnt to value more than anything in my life, and which I could ill afford to lose. So hopeless, till this instant, have I been of ever obtaining more."

"Why?" asked Roma.

"Why?" he repeated. "For the reason I have already told you, and for another. Think of my position! A struggling engineer—an artisan, some of your people would call me, I daresay; for I am not yet at the top of my tree by any means, nor likely to be so for many a long day to come. The only home I can offer my wife is an unattractive one enough—you know what sort of a place Wareborough is—is that the home *you* are suited to? You, beautiful, courted, admired; spoilt by every sort of rule you should be, but I don't think you are. I am not exactly poor, certainly, but I am not rich, and there is hard work before me for years to come. There now, Miss Eyrecourt, you know the whole. I have great reason to be sanguine of success, have I not?"

"And this is all?" she said. "You have told me every one of the 'insuperable obstacles?'"

"Every one," he replied. "Don't torture me, Roma."

She held out both her hands; she lifted up her beautiful face and looked at him with tears in her large soft dark eyes. "Oh, Gerald," she said at last, when the two hands were pressed closely in his, when she felt his gaze of almost incredulous joy fixed upon her with eager questioning; "Oh, Gerald, how could you mistake me so? 'Spoilt,' am I? Ah no, or if so, not by the excess of love that has been lavished on me. I have been very lonely; it is years and years since I have known what it was to have a home—a real home. Even had I not loved you, I confess to you the temptation of *your* love, your strength and protection, would have been great to me. You don't know what to me would have been the mere thought of having some one I could perfectly trust. But as it is, I needn't think of temptation. I love you, Gerald. I would rather have your 'poor battered old heart' than anything in the universe. And if this makes amends for the dilapidated state of yours, I can assure you that mine, such as it is, is quite whole. I give it to you entirely, without the slightest little chip or crack."

She had begun to speak with the tears in her eyes; as she went on, notwithstanding her half-joking tone, they dropped—one, two, three big tears. She pulled away one hand to dash them aside, but Gerald caught it, kissed it tenderly and gratefully, and held it fast again.

"Roma," he said, "you and your heart are far too good for me. My darling, how shall I ever repay the sacrifices you will make for me? Are you sure, quite sure, you will never repent it? Have you considered it all? Think of having to live at Wareborough."

"Gerald, you are too bad! Do you know you have all but driven me into proposing to you? I shall think *you* repent your bargain if you say much more. Living at

Wareborough! Nonsense. I should be quite pleased and content to live in a coal mine with *you*. There now, I am not going to spoil you by any more pretty speeches, which, by rights, sir, please to remember, should come from the other side."

With such encouragement, Mr. Thurston, considering it was the first time he had actually tried his hand at anything of the kind, acquitted himself very fairly, and the remaining two miles of their walk seemed to them but a small fraction of the real distance. They had time, however, to discuss a good many aspects of their plans. "What would Frank and Sydney think? how astonished they would be!" "How pleased Eugenia would feel!" &c., &c. before they re-entered the park and came within sight of the house.

They approached it from one side, intending, however, to enter by the front door. What was it, as they drew near, that gave Roma an indescribable feeling that something had happened since they went out? She could not have told. The hall door was half open for one thing, but it was not that. It was a so-called "instinct"—one of those subtile revelations which science has not yet learnt to define or explain by any thoroughly apprehended law.

There was hardly time for even the realisation of a fear. The wave of vague apprehension had hardly ruffled the girl's happy spirit when it was confirmed. The hall door opened a little wider, a little figure, evidently on the watch, rushed out.

"Aunty Woma," cried Floss, flinging herself into Miss Eyrecourt's arms, forgetful of the certain amount of awe with which Roma still inspired her, regardless of the awful presence of Mr. Thurston; "Aunty Woma, something dweadful has happened. The ponies has wunned away, and little Tim has wunned home to tell. Uncle Beachey is killed quite dead on the dot, Tim says, and I don't know where Aunty 'Genia is."

"What does she say?" asked Gerald, hoarsely.

"Tell him; say it again, Floss," said Roma, forcing her pale lips to move; and as well as she could, for her sobs, the child repeated her ghastly tale.

Without another word, Mr. Thurston rushed off, and in an instant was lost to Roma's sight among the thick growing shrubs that lay in the direction of the stables. What became of Floss her aunt never knew; probably in her intense anxiety to know more, the child followed the person whom she imagined most likely to obtain further information. However that may have been, Roma found herself alone—alone with this strange dreamlike feeling of horror and grief for Beauchamp's untimely fate, which it never occurred to her to doubt —alone with a yet more terrible companion. What was the meaning of this sudden misery which overwhelmed her? Whence had come this poisonous suggestion which, so marvellously speedy is the growth of thought, had, even while the child was speaking, sprung to life in her brain? Beauchamp dead, Eugenia free, and the words which her newly made lover had spoken not an hour before ringing in her ears:

"If she had not married it would have been different. I believe I should have gone on hoping——"

How would it be now? What should she do? Oh, if only she had not encouraged him to say more, for without encouragement, now whispered the serpent in her heart, he would certainly not have said so much.

"Good God," thought poor Roma, in her anguish and self-horror, "what a selfish wretch I am! What shall I do? How shall I bear it?"

The words uttered aloud recalled her somewhat to herself. She was hastening to the house, intent on burying self at least for the present—on seeing in what way she could be of use to others, when Mr. Thurston suddenly re-appeared. He came out by the hall door, hastened up to her quickly but without speaking. He was deadly pale, and when close beside her he seemed to move his lips once or twice before any sound was audible. Then at last he spoke.

"Roma," he said, "wait a moment. There is no hurry. Everything has been done. They have sent for doctors and all. It," he stopped, and seemed to gasp for breath, "it happened near the Chilworth lodge. I am just going there. I only came out to tell you. Floss's version was not quite correct. Roma," he stopped again, "it is even worse—forgive me, I cannot help saying so—it is not Beauchamp. It—it is Eugenia?"

The last words were hardly audible, they came with a sort of a sob. For once in his life Gerald was utterly unmanned. But Roma heard them only too plainly.

"Eugenia!" she cried, her voice rising almost into a scream; "oh no, Mr. Thurston, not Eugenia. You do not mean she is *dead?* Say, oh, do say it is a mistake," she clasped her hands together in wild entreaty; "you *must* say it is a mistake."

He looked at her with unutterable pity, but shook his head.

"I cannot say so," he replied; "from what I was told it seems only too certain. But I am going there at once. Will you come? no, perhaps you had better not. I will let you know immediately what I find. It *may* not be so bad. Roma, dearest Roma, do not lose heart so."

He would have put his arm round her, but she eluded his grasp.

"Don't touch me," she said, wildly, "you don't know how wicked I am. It is true—I feel it is true. Oh, Eugenia! God forgive me. I think my punishment is greater than I can bear," and before her lover could stop her she had rushed into the house.

For a moment Gerald gazed after her in distress and bewilderment, half doubting if he had heard aright.

"She does not know what she is saying," he decided. "My poor Roma, the shock has been too much for her; but I cannot stay," and at a rapid pace he set off across the park in the direction of the scene of the frightful disaster.

Upstairs, meanwhile, Roma, locked into her own room, "matter-of-fact, easy-going" Roma—Roma, "into whose composition entered no tragic elements," Gerald

Thurston's light-hearted betrothed of one short hour ago, was passing through an agony of remorse, a very fiery furnace of misery, such as falls to the lot of few women of her healthy, happy nature.

CHAPTER X.

FROM THE GATES OF THE GRAVE.

"The best is yet to be,
The last of life, for which the first was made:
Our times are in His hand,
Who saith 'A whole I planed,
Youth shows but half: see all, nor be afraid!'"
RABBI BEN EZRA.

SHE was not dead. "Still alive, but perfectly unconscious," was the report that met Gerald as he reached the lodge. "They have not told Captain Chancellor how bad it is," added Mr. Thurston's informant, "for he was severely stunned himself, and the hearing it might do him harm. He thinks Mrs. Chancellor escaped unhurt."

A little later Gerald caught a glimpse of the Chilworth surgeon. This gentleman seemed glad to get hold of some responsible person.

"Mrs. Chancellor's brother-in-law, Mr.

Thurston, I presume," he began, and Gerald did not think the slight mistake worth correcting. "I have sent to Chilworth to telegraph for Dr. Frobisher, of Marley. I suppose I did right?"

"Most certainly," answered Gerald.

"You see I had no one to consult—we must keep it from Captain Chancellor as long as possible, he has had a narrow escape himself—and I feel the responsibility very great. There is no wonder they thought Mrs. Chancellor was killed, at first—I almost thought so myself when I first came."

"Then what is your opinion now?" Gerald ventured to ask, fancying a shadow of hope was inferred by the surgeon's manner.

"I think there is a slight hope, a very slight one. It will hang on a thread for some days at the best, but she is young and very healthy, though not strong. If she escapes, however, it will be little short of a miracle. Can you tell me how it happened? It seems an extraordinary thing altogether; the ponies were not wild, the coachman tells me, and had been driven several times."

Gerald told what he knew. The ponies, it appeared, from the boy Timothy's account, had gone beautifully, "as quiet as quiet," all the way, till on their return home Beauchamp had stopped for a moment at the lodge to get a light for his cigar. There was no man in the house; only the lodge-keeper's wife was at home, and she unfortunately, encumbered with a screaming baby who would scarcely allow her to open the gate. Captain Chancellor, to save her trouble, jumped out of the carriage, giving the reins to his wife, and calling to Tim to stand by the ponies' heads. The boy was on the point of obeying, when his mistress told him to stay where he was; " She could hold them quite well, she said," was the child's account, "and she thought they should learn to stand still of theirselves." It was an unfortunate experiment; the ponies, eager to reach their stable, were irritated by the delay almost within sight of their home. They began to fret and fidget, and Eugenia, by way of soothing them, walked them on slowly a few paces. Then something, what, no one ever knew (possibly only the animals' own unrestrainable impatience), startled them, and with a desperate plunge they dashed forward just as their master came out of the lodge. There was a rush and a scramble, which Tim could not clearly describe. He remembered seeing Captain Chancellor dart forward, catch hold of the reins on the side nearest to him, and for a moment the boy thought they were saved. Only for a moment, however; it seemed to him his master was dragged a few yards, then kicked violently aside, "all of a heap, he lay without moving," said the boy. "I thought he was killed, and so did my mistress. She stood up in the carriage and screamed out 'he is killed, it is my fault,' and then in another minute she were out too. I don't know if she throwed herself out or not; the carriage shook so, going so fast and she standing up, she could hardly have kep' in." Apparently Tim thought it his duty to throw himself after her. He confessed to the idea having crossed his mind, but remembered no more till he woke up to find himself shaken and confused, though otherwise unhurt, some twenty yards or so from the spot where the first part of the catastrophe had occurred. The ponies, satisfied, seemingly, with their day's work, pursued their way home, their pace gradually subsiding as they became conscious of being their own masters. They rattled into the courtyard, no one at the first sound of their approach suspecting anything amiss, till the first glance of the empty carriage, and the torn and dragging reins told their own dreadful tale.

Such was the explanation of the accident. Mr. Benyon listened in silence, shook his head when Gerald finished speaking, and then went back to his patient again to await the arrival of the greater man from Marley.

Gerald lost no time in sharing with Roma the crumb of comfort he had found.

"It is not quite so bad as I was told at first. She is still alive, but there is very little hope. Will you not come? There is nothing to do. She is perfectly unconscious, but I think it would be less wretched for you than staying up there alone. Tell poor little Floss we hope her aunt will soon be better."

This was the pencilled note—Roma's first letter from her lover, a sad enough one truly—which Mr. Thurston sent to the poor girl, waiting in all the anguish of well-nigh hopeless anxiety for his report. Within half-an-hour she had joined him, pale, haggard, careworn, aged even it almost seemed, from the bright Roma of an hour or two ago, but calm, self-possessed now, ready for any service that might be required of her. And the sweet summer afternoon deepened into sweeter evening; the moon shone out in cold indifferent loveliness; here and there through the latticed windows of the cottage a star peeped in with its cheery twinkle, and still the dreary vigil went on; still lay on the pallet bed where they had first carried her, the so lately beautiful form of Eugenia Chancellor, beautiful still, but with a death-like beauty that seemed already to separate her from the living breathing beings about her. Only from time to time she moaned faintly, and moved her head from side to side uneasily on the pillow with the sad restlessness so pitiful to see; telling too surely to the experienced eye of invisible injury to the delicate brain.

It was unspeakably painful to witness, knowing that so little could be done to relieve or mitigate the suffering. And not the least painful part of what Roma and her lover had to go through, was the sight of Beauchamp Chancellor's suffering when the truth as to Eugenia was broken to him. His distress was indescribable; so evidentlo genuine in its depth that more than once in the course of the next few days Roma found herself asking herself if, after all her many years' knowledge of him, she had done full justice to his capacity for true and earnest feeling, to the latent possibilities for good in his character below the crust of worldliness and selfishness. Or was it that he had altered and improved, that contact with a nature so fresh and genuine and single-minded as Eugenia's, had done its work; that notwithstanding her many faults and mistakes, the essential beauty of her sweetness and simplicity had unconsciously asserted itself, had found a little-suspected vein of sympathy in the lower nature of her husband? It almost seemed as if it were so, and if so, oh how sad, how doubly to be regretted, the premature ending of the fair young life so full of promise, so prized and precious.

"She has been so much happier lately, Roma," poor Beauchamp would say, in his yearning for consolation and sympathy. "She was saying so herself just the other day. I am a coarse selfish creature compared with her. No one but I knows thoroughly how innocent, and true, and unselfish she is, and I took a long time to find it out—I can't forgive myself when I think of that time—but lately I do think I have got to understand her better, and to make her happier. Don't you think so, Roma? *She* said so herself, you know."

And Roma would agree with him, and say whatever she could think of in the way of comfort—a dozen times a day, for Beauchamp followed her about in a touchingly helpless, dependent sort of manner, as if in her presence alone he found his anxiety endurable. A dozen times a day, too, he would appeal to whichever doctor was on the spot, almost entreating for a word of hope or comfort. "I fancy she is lying more quietly just now," he would say; or, "Don't you think the expression of her face is calmer, more like itself?"

It was very hard to be unable to agree with him, but weary days, and still wearier nights, went by before either doctors or friends thought it would be any but cruel kindness to allow him to hope. At last, however—a long of coming "at last" it was—there crept into sight the first faint flutter of improvement; slowly, very slowly, life and consciousness returned to the all but dying wife, and after a new phase of anxiety, scarcely less trying than the first, the verdict was pronounced, "There is hope—the greatest danger to be apprehended in the way of recovery has been safely past—there is every reasonable ground for hope." And then, hour by hour, day by day, week by week, Eugenia crept back to her place in the world, to the place which it had seemed all but certain would be vacant for evermore. Her extreme patience, her tranquil gentleness, had much to do with her recovery, said the authorities. And those who knew her best—Gerald and Roma, and Sydney when she came—knew her excitable impetuosity, her impatience of inaction, marvelled somewhat at this new revelation of her character.

"You are so good, Eugenia," said Roma, one day when she was alone with the patient, still forced to lie motionless and unemployed, forbidden even to use her eyes or to talk much. "I cannot think how you have learnt to bear these long weeks of suffering, or at least tedium, so cheerfully."

Eugenia drew her friend's head down

close beside her on her pillow. "Don't you see, dear Roma," she whispered, "how easy it is for me to be patient now that I am so happy? There has not been any suffering too much for me; I am so selfish that I cannot even regret the anxiety you all went through about me, for think what it has brought me—as nothing else could have done—the full knowledge of Beauchamp's love. Never, since the dreadful day when first I doubted it, have I felt so assured of it as since this accident; never, since the passing away of my unreal, unreasonable dreams, has life looked so sweet to me as now, for though I know now that troubles, and disappointment, and failure *must* come; though I dare say I shall often feel them bitterly and exaggeratedly, still I can never again feel hopeless or heartless—I can never feel that my life has no value or object."

Roma kissed her silently, but did not speak. In a minute or two Eugenia spoke again—

"And if anything was wanting to make me still happier, to make me more grateful for this new return to life, it is what you have told me about yourself and Gerald," she said affectionately. "You are both so wise and good, you have both been so wise and good in what you have done for me, that I cannot tell you how happy I am in your happiness. Happiness actually in your grasp, with real root and foundation. You will not have to travel to it through vanished illusions as I did;" she sighed a little. "But I was hot-headed, and wilful, and selfish, and so I blinded myself. *You* have always thought of others more than of yourself, Roma. You have been reasonable and patient all your life. You deserve to step straight into happiness."

"No I don't, Eugenia. No one but I myself knows how little I deserve it," whispered Roma. But she said no more, and Eugenia accepted her words simply as the expression of her womanly humility.

"Her engagement to Gerald has improved her in the only respect improvement in her —in my eyes at least—was possible," thought Eugenia. "It has softened her so wonderfully. No one could call her too self-confident or decided in manner now."

But Roma in her own heart felt herself more changed than others suspected.

"I prided myself on my high principle and superiority to low influences, jealousy and selfishness, and all such unworthy feelings. And I fancied, too, I had so much self-command, even in thought," she said to her lover, sadly, when, after Eugenia was fairly out of danger, she confessed to him the cruel storm of feeling, the anguish of self-reproach through which she had passed the day of the accident; "and see what I am in reality! Imagine the horrible, the repulsive selfishness of my feeling as I did at such a time, even for an instant."

"But it was partly my fault," said Gerald. "I had expressed myself badly. Don't you see how it was? I was so afraid of deceiving you in any way, of in the least concealing from you what I *had* felt for another woman (though indeed you knew it already) that I misrepresented it. I mixed up past and present. Thinking it over since, indeed, I wonder you didn't refuse to have anything to say to me. I don't feel proud of my way of expressing myself that afternoon, I assure you."

"I told you at the time you very nearly made me propose to you," said Roma, half laughing in spite of her seriousness.

"But you misunderstood me, you did indeed," he persisted. "I hardly like to talk about it, but to speak plainly, my love for Eugenia died, completely and for ever, the day I first learnt to think of her as the wife, the promised or actual wife—it all seemed one to me—of another. Had there been no other in the question, had it been a simple question of winning her by long devotion to care for me, I don't say what limits there would have been to my perseverance. But as it was——"

"Don't explain," interrupted Roma. "I don't want you to explain. It can't make me feel myself the least bit less despicable. I that have always despised other women so for being run away with by their feelings, even good ones. Oh, Gerald, are you sure you wouldn't rather give me up now you know how bad I am?"

He smiled.

"Do you remember how I offended you long, long ago," he said, "by persisting that you were no judge of your own character? Even then, at first sight, I doubted your belonging to the easy-going, prosaic order of beings you declared yourself to be one of. There are doubtless in all of us," he went on more gravely, after a little pause, "*possibilities* of evil, of selfishness—the root of it all, I suppose, but I am no metaphysician—which we may well tremble to recognise. And in the lurid light of tempests of feeling, these are apt to show themselves in exaggerated blackness and enormity. But you cannot think, Roma, that I would love you less for seeing more of the depth of your character, the depth, and the strength, and the truth of it?" he added, tenderly.

So Roma was comforted. And Eugenia's prediction that her two friends would "step straight into happiness," was fulfilled as thoroughly as any prophecy of the kind can be fulfilled in a world where so very many things are crooked, more crooked than needs be, because so very few people have faith and patience sufficient to await the slow-coming, far-off, eventual "making straight" —faith and patience enough to work cheerily meanwhile in their own corner of the great vineyard. For though the tools be poor and imperfect, the soil hard, the light dim and fitful, oftentimes indeed delusive, the results of the labour all but invisible, what then?

> "Is not our failure here but a triumph's evidence
> For the fulness of the days?"

THE END.

LONDON:
SAVILL, EDWARDS AND CO., PRINTERS, CHANDOS STREET,
COVENT GARDEN.